T H E   B E A C H   B O Y S :

S I L V E R   A N N I V E R S A R Y

T   H   E

BEACH BOYS SILVER ANNIVERSARY

TEXT BY JOHN MILWARD

DESIGN BY J. C. SUARÉS

PHOTOS EDITED BY ILENE CHERNA

PRODUCTION BY CAROLINE GINESI

A DOLPHIN BOOK
DOUBLEDAY & COMPANY, INC.
GARDEN CITY, NEW YORK
1985

Library of Congress Cataloging in Publication Data

Milward, John.
   The Beach Boys silver anniversary.

   "A Dolphin book."
   Discography: pp. 234–36
   1. Beach Boys.   2. Rock musicians—United States—
Biography.   I. Title.
ML421.B38M5   1985   784.5′4′00924 [B] 84-21112
ISBN: 0-385-19650-4

Roll down the window, put down the top
Crank up the Beach Boys, baby
Don't let the music stop
We're gonna ride it till we just can't ride it no more

Randy Newman, "I Love L.A."

INDEPENDENCE DAY, 1984, AND ON THE CEREMONIAL MALL IN Washington, D.C., over a quarter of a million Americans have come to celebrate the birth of the nation with a free concert by the Beach Boys. Parents who were themselves kids when the Beach Boys bounded out of Southern California in 1962 with an invitation to join a surfin' safari have brought their young children. Large groups of teenagers pretend they're at the beach, sprawling on blankets with coolers of beer on each corner. All they know about the Beach Boys, who on this day will perform almost nothing recorded after 1966, are the old hits, but that doesn't seem to matter—these songs speak to and from a teenage sensibility that remains constant. The boys still horse around, trying to impress the girls, who giggle among themselves and steal glances at the boys.

The story of the Beach Boys is one of music and family, heroes and villains, fathers and sons. It tells of California and an ethos of perpetual fun that America successively embraced, ridiculed, and then embraced again. It is the tale of three brothers, a cousin, and a high school friend, their meteoric rise to stardom in the nascent days of modern rock and roll, and their long and torturous fall within a pop world that they couldn't have imagined. The story of the Beach Boys is also the singular tale of Brian Wilson, who created the songs that gave us summer and buckled under the burdens of his own artistry. And finally it is the evolution of a body of work that has transcended the blood and tears that went into its making.

"Brian Wilson is the Beach Boys," said his brother Dennis. "He is the band. We're his messengers." The message, stripped to its bone, was that summer means fun and in California the fun never stops. Brian created a California dream for those locked between the two oceans, and his music transported teen-

---

Brian Douglas Wilson.

age America to a special place where balmy Saturday afternoons stretched out into an endless July. Where Elvis Presley introduced young whites to the forbidden fruits theretofore hidden within the folds of America's multiracial culture, Brian Wilson and the Beach Boys sparked their early sixties constituency by celebrating the kids' own culture. There was no condescension in the songs of the Beach Boys—if they were trifling tales of drag races and school spirit, they were handled in a manner that neither overwhelmed nor belittled their subject. The Beach Boys simply amplified the fun that was the province of the American teenager.

Brian's work proved that teenage music needn't be a pejorative term and that one could employ innovative stylistic motifs without necessarily overburdening adolescent themes. Musically, his greatest contribution was the pioneering use of complex vocal harmonies within a rock band format. The Beach Boys sang in round, clean tones with relatively little vibrato, and the result was that their voices blended into a silken sheen wherein it was sometimes difficult to identify the individual singers. The stylistic roots of the Beach Boys go back to madrigal church music of the Middle Ages—music written for three or more voices, usually without instrumental accompaniment, though Brian wasn't one to pore over yellowed manuscripts. He simply came to similar conclusions. Still, an intriguing parallel exists between the harmonic singers of old and the scrubbed white Protestant kids who emerged from Hawthorne. Before the madrigal style was written into the musical liturgy, it was the oral tradition of troubadours, who after all were the pop singers of their day. The Beach Boys, then, were sophisticated troubadours of untroubled times who sang with a passion rooted in the gospel. Or, as Carl Wilson would have it, "Brian's whole thing all along—his grand obsession, if you like—has been the juxtaposition of the dumb and the brilliant."

Alan Charles Jardine.

There was more to Brian Wilson, however, than a blind infatuation with fun. In truth, he was the shy outsider, at once appreciative of the ability to lose oneself in the moment and fearful of the dangerous intimacy that such spontaneity invites. Brian's upbeat teen fantasies were a reflection of life as he would have liked to live it; more characteristic of his actual frame of mind were the ballads, and it is here, as much as in his songs of frivolity, that he taps the teenage heart.

In 1984 a twenty-year-old Italian man, macho to the max, carries a cassette player into a session with his female therapist. "You probably don't know this song," he says, punching on the recorder, "but it's about me. I play it under my covers every night." And suddenly there's Brian, singing from his heart, from his soul, from 1963's "In My Room." "There's a world," he sings, "where I can go," quiet and holy, "and tell my secrets to." He's joined by the voices of his imagination, his family, his group: "In my room." The therapist smiles a deep, rich smile, and suddenly she's a teenage girl: "I kissed my first boy to this song."

The key three-letter word in describing the thematic thrust of the Beach Boys is "fun," but there is another three-letter word that is equally significant in the context of their story: "sad." A case could be made that Brian was never happier than when he was a teenager hiding out and discovering his instinctive talent for music-making. Surely, there were mitigating factors that sent him scurrying into his room—first and foremost a violent father who instilled in Brian a profound need to excel but lacked the sensitivity to reward his efforts with unfettered love. Murry Wilson's dream was to succeed as a musician; his firstborn's ambition was to please his father. Music came naturally for Brian, and in the kind of tragic twist that perverts the love between a father and son, that was one thing that Murry could not forgive.

Dennis Carl Wilson.

Brian's gift transformed his family—he became the father-provider, and made them all rich. In the early years, as he and the Beach Boys used his burgeoning talents to sketch a happy teenage wonderland, the world was their milkshake. But there comes a time when a boy must become a man. Brian had found great success within an adolescent context, but as he moved into his mid-twenties he felt the need to go beyond lyrics of cars and girls. Brian's adventurous mid-sixties music alienated the Beach Boys' teenage audience, and some critics contend that it was folly to think that he could find themes as universally compelling as those of teenage fun. Others believe that *Pet Sounds* lifted pop music to a whole new plateau, and that the best was yet to come. We'll never know—as soon as the public bucked, the Beach Boys backed down and left Brian without the support system that had allowed him to excel. For Brian's group, sophistication was fine as long as it sold as much as "Fun, Fun, Fun."

Brian reached his commercial and artistic peak with the 1966 release of the Beach Boys' "Good Vibrations," and promptly fell to pieces. Drugs, increased tensions within the group, and an artistic drive that was at once fueled and burned out by five years of extraordinary productivity left him, at the age of twenty-five, a man-child doomed to failure. "I think he got caught in a trap with 'Good Vibrations,'" says Phil Spector, the first record producer to put an auteur's stamp on rock and roll, and a youthful success whose own story bears a striking similarity to Brian's. "He became a prisoner instead of a poet." Brian Wilson was reborn a legendary rock and roll casualty, and for the past eighteen years has lived in the shadow of a catalog of music that has brought generations of Americans great joy. He became the flaw in his own wondrous myth—the unhappy man in a world of perpetual fun.

I first saw the Beach Boys in 1964 at the Westchester County Center, and

Michael Edward Love.

the only thing I can remember is those red-striped shirts. Judging by my tattered copy of *Shut Down* Vol. 2 and the orange-and-yellow 45s that dot my record collection, it's clear that I was already singing along. I've never stopped, though by 1975, when in a new role of critic I watched the Beach Boys turn the Chicago Stadium into a shaking pavilion of nostalgic celebration, my perspective had changed. Sing as I might, it was clear that the public laundering of Brian's psychological problems had thrown a permanent pall over the innocent pleasures of his music. To love the Beach Boys is to know that the flip side of happy is sad. Ten years later Dennis Wilson is dead, and the songs remain the same.

In preparing this manuscript I immersed myself in the music of the Beach Boys, became reacquainted with many old friends, and gained a renewed appreciation for the timelessness of Brian's songs and innovative productions. I caught three live shows in as many months: a New York City charity revue in which Brian made me squirm with his one hoarse verse of "Surfer Girl" and Mike Love made me angry with his patronizing introduction of the man who made him famous; an outdoor show in Monterey, California, where Frisbees arced in the sunlit Pacific breeze while the band played on automatic pilot; and the Washington, D.C., extravaganza, where I once again swallowed hard as Carl and Bruce Johnston combined to sing Brian's lead to "Don't Worry Baby." That afternoon in Washington, Brian sat at an electric piano playing the songs of his young and gifted life. Brian is in his mid-40s now, and he hasn't written a major hit tune in over a dozen years, yet still, he's a giant. In five years he conjured a lifetime of fun, and the Beach Boys have made that vision live for a quarter century. I shook Brian's hand that day and thanked him for me, as well as for you.

Carl Dean Wilson.

ECEMBER 1961, IN A PLACE WHERE IT'S NEVER really winter, Southern California. The Wilson brothers—Brian, Dennis, and Carl—pile out of the house at the corner of 119th and Kornblum and climb into Brian's 1957 Ford. Dennis, as usual, wants to go to the beach. Carl favors Foster's Freeze. Brian turns on the radio, carefully navigates the car onto 120th Street, and suggests that they stop for shakes on the way to Manhattan Beach. Caught dawdling by a red light, Brian watches a prop jet make its languorous descent toward the Oriental airline terminal. By the time he turns onto Hawthorne Boulevard, everybody's singing along with the Hollywood Argyles—"Alley Oop, oop, oop, oop-oop"—until they're suddenly yanked up and out the window by the deejay's electrifying announcement: "Here's a group from Hawthorne: the Beach Boys." The car jerks and jolts to a stop as "Surfin'"—*their* song, *Brian's* song—jumps out of the dashboard. The Beach Boys—Brian, Dennis, Carl, Mike Love, and Al Jardine—had quietly climbed atop the wave of a lifetime. Radio blasting, they drank in the sound like green plants taking the sun or children blushing with approval. According to Dennis, he ran down the street screaming, Carl threw up, and Brian's eyes shone with a pure white light.

California may have meant the end of American elbowroom, but it at least offered pioneers a fresh new horizon. Here the continental sun sank last and plopped down flat into the Pacific. California inspired all sorts of dreamers—prospectors who scuttled across the prairie in the great Gold Rush, garment men who sixty years later found treasure in the hills of Hollywood, and a postwar population that was drawn from the cold industrial North to the hub of the Sun Belt. Boomtown, a fresh start, no roots. In the hot flush of passion

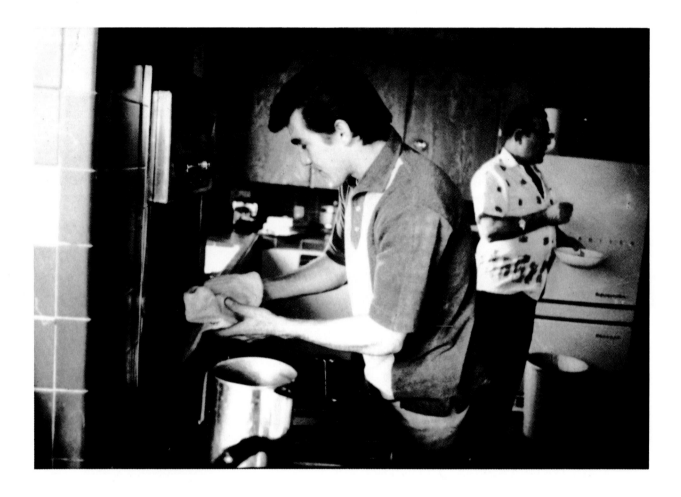

Dennis and Murry fix a snack in the kitchen of the
Wilsons' Hawthorne home, located at 3701 West
119th Street.

Brian picnicking with high school chum Rich Sloan.
Says Sloan: "Nothing really serious was Brian's way
of doing things. His nature was just to be honest,
play fair, play hard, and enjoy it for what it's
worth."

OVERLEAF:

Brian watching the fun at Senior Ditch Day during the
spring of 1960. Perhaps he's worried about the
durability of the "invisible" ink that Rich Sloan had
splashed on his shirt.

Brian (second from left) performing with friends at a
high school assembly. Though Brian was in the
twelfth grade, the group was not called the Four
Seniors.

that followed the Big War, families were begun and the economy met the expectations of a consumer society that was busy being born. The suburban tract houses that spread from Long Island to Santa Barbara were a vision of sunny normalcy as clean and Christian as their closely cropped lawns. Gatsby looked out into the Atlantic toward the Old World and saw a red light—and the end of the American Dream. The rest of America looked west, into the Pacific and the newest of the New World. And the light was green.

The Beach Boys made music that perpetuated an image of California as an everyday Disneyland of cars, girls, and so much fun that you had to say it three times. In California, went this belief, everything was bright and colorful, like on television or in the movies. The good life, the real good life. California's show-biz culture created a diverse set of Hollywood dreams, but they all

Brian (right) with high school friend Ted Sprague,
getting physical with two of the Beach Boys' favorite
subjects: cars and water.

referred back East. The movies brought their source material and style from the world of New York publishing and theater—and their history from Europe. TV paid its tab by being the advertising mouthpiece of Madison Avenue. The music business, however, remained a largely East Coast phenomenon, with songs written by hungry hired guns and sung by grateful teens whose managers smoked Cuban cigars and got them on "American Bandstand."

The Beach Boys were children of the fifties who, with the charisma of the kids next door, became suburban American troubadours for a last-gasp age of innocence. Coming of age just after Alaska and Hawaii became states, they took their inspiration—quite literally—from looking west. Along with producer Phil Spector, but with a decidedly more Californian cant, they established Los Angeles as a pop music power. Later for paradise on the fault line, where fun in the sun can turn into after-dinner drinks with Charlie Manson and where months without rain prepare the reclaimed desert for brutal brushfires. The Beach Boys reflected only the good stuff: french fries and Frisbees, summer days (and summer nights).

Murry Wilson, the father of the Beach Boys, was a typical resident of Los Angeles—he had arrived in the city when he was nine years old. His family hadn't come from Kansas with stars in their eyes, but they knew it couldn't be worse than the dusty Depression of the Midwest. California had mountains to the east, the Pacific to the west, and there was no such thing as smog. The Korthoffs moved to L.A. from Minneapolis when their daughter Audree was ten. Murry met Audree at Washington High School, they harmonized, and in 1938, when they were both twenty, married.

In the early forties, Los Angeles was sketched alongside the Hollywood hills, running westward from Griffith Park to Santa Monica. The San Fernando Valley and Orange County, dominated by long stretches of citrus groves, were sprinkled with rural outposts. Wartime industry, particularly the aeronautics concerns clustered around the airport in Inglewood, brought quick growth to the southland. Murry worked for Goodyear, lost an eye in an industrial accident, and started his own small company, ABLE Machinery, that leased heavy equipment. Brian Douglas was the first born (June 20, 1942), followed by Dennis Carl (December 4, 1944). The young family moved to Hawthorne, a mostly white, lower middle-class community near the airport and five miles from the ocean. The birth of Carl Dean (December 21, 1946) filled the five-room house, and the three boys shared a room, giggling under the covers, and later, singing themselves to sleep. And as they grew, so did Los Angeles, rolling up the hills and into the valley to become a horizon of endless suburbs.

Murry was not happy with machinery; he fancied himself a musician and was happiest at the piano, singing and writing songs, or playing duets with Audree on the organ. Murry got his songs published, but never had much luck selling them. He once recorded a demo of one of his songs, and played it endlessly. The first song that Brian can remember, from age two, was *Rhapsody in Blue.* He learned to play the accordion by ear. In church he was the boy soprano, soloing on "We Three Kings of Orient Are," but when he'd sing in school, the kids would make fun of his high, sweet voice. Brian felt naked, embarrassed, and would learn to keep his music, his gift, close to his heart. He'd lock himself in his adolescent bedroom—actually the family music room, fashioned from a converted garage—and turn the radio on to KFWB. Sitting at the piano, Brian would dismantle the cool, white harmonies of California pop and put them back together. He'd learn the parts of one, two, and finally all Four Freshmen. Sometimes Brian and Audree would sing two-part Freshmen songs into a tape recorder, play them back, and add the other two voices. Carl, who was the son closest to Audree, would occasionally add a third voice. Dennis was always somewhere else, usually at the beach, and he paid for his independence.

"My father had a unique way of showing his affection," said Dennis, many times, "which consisted of beating the shit out of us." Murry demanded the best of everybody, especially himself, and the whole family took the heat when somebody, especially Murry, came up short. Audree was caught in the middle; Carl kept quiet. Dennis bore the brunt of Murry's wrath—brutal beatings, sometimes in public—and rebelled from the beginning. Brian begged for approval, pulling down A's and B's in school and becoming a bona fide jock on the athletic field, but he came in a close second. "It made me feel like I was inferior," Brian has said. "It made me feel worthless." One story has Murry humiliating Brian by forcing him to defecate on a newspaper. Another has Brian dumping it on a plate and serving it to Murry for dinner. But the most hurtful stories feature Brian speculating on how he came to have only 6 percent hearing in his right ear: "Ever since I was born—or maybe, when I was two years old, somebody punched me in the ear." Only Brian, who has never heard stereo and who became one of pop music's greatest producers anyway, could find the smile in this sad, fearful web. When Murry ordered his son to tell *Rolling Stone* that none of this was true, Brian replied, "I'll tell you what. Let's tell them that I shit in your ear and you hit me in the head with a plate."

Harmony. In a house that was either soothed by song or racked by violence, Brian became obsessed with harmony. He could imagine a handful of melodies in his head, sing one, and hear the rest of them, poised and pretty. Brian was open to all music—it would have been difficult, for one thing, to be Carl's brother and not like Chuck Berry—but what thrilled him the most was the cerebral hum put out by the blending of voices. Mix two sounds, Brian was learning, and you have a third. The earth could be quaking, but if, say, the Fleetwoods' "Come Softly to Me" was on the radio, Brian would die singing . . . and happy. He knew he couldn't say it, because it was so stupid, but just a couple of voices could sound almost spiritual. He and his cousin, Mike Love, the son of Audree's sister, would sit in the car late at night, singing harmonies

Brian added the wild honey to the vocal sound of the Beach Boys. He loved performing onstage, as it gave him license to sing in the falsetto that had brought him the taunts of his schoolmates.

with the radio. Mike went to a different, funkier high school and was moved most by the blue notes of rhythm and blues. Mike gave Brian a foundation—the bass "dom-dom, dom-da-dom, lu-be-do" of "Come Softly to Me"—for something that didn't yet exist: suburban doo-wop.

"C'mon, let's twist again!" In the early sixties, silly dance crazes notwithstanding, adults generally had their thing and kids had quite another. There was no such thing as a youth culture, just a bunch of kids, and kids were kids until they were no longer teenagers. Parents breathed easy—with James Dean dead and Elvis in the army, there weren't even any young-punk heroes to fear—and kids lived for fun. Teenage cool was a blue-moon expression of lots of money. Teen dollars had flooded a newly born category of American business—the leisure industry—and fathers worked so that their families could spend. California, where fads sizzle on an open grill night and day, was leisure city, simply *the* place to be a kid. Sunshine, hot rods, and fifteen-cent hamburgers. "Kookie, Kookie, lend me your comb." Girls, girls, girls. And the

During a British TV appearance, Dennis, looking like the Beach Boys' answer to the Rolling Stones' Brian Jones, checks out the gear.

Brian keeps warm while playing some cool bass riffs during the same BBC taping. Like Beatle Paul, Brian was the onstage bassist.

waves, always the waves, calling out along the shore with all the froth and fury that is California. These are waves that demand to be ridden, and the kid that climbs atop a big one, and hangs down deep inside its pipeline, is on top of the world.

Dennis was a surfer. As a toddler, he would stare out the front door for hours as if waiting for his legs to take him away. Soon enough he'd be out the door, down the block, and on the beach. He was a tough kid—a loner—and prone to fights. Murry beat him and Dennis took it outside the house. While the family sang, Dennis would be having some kind of adventure—dangerous, no doubt. He was the last of the Wilson brothers to become interested in music, banging out boogie-woogie piano at those rare times when Brian wouldn't be commanding the keys. Carl was attracted to the guitar, taking lessons and imagining himself ringing his guitar just like Johnny B. Goode. Murry was pleased that his sons shared his love of music, although he couldn't abide by their taste, and was piqued that Brian, who would create new arrangements for every two-bit hit he heard on the radio, didn't want to sing his father's songs. Still, one fine day Murry took Brian to see a concert by the Four Freshmen, and after wrangling backstage access, the father introduced the singers to his red-faced first son.

The individual Beach Boys never played in active teenage bands, though Brian was known to sing in high school assemblies. Otherwise, except for oddities like youth night at the Angeles Mesa Presbyterian Church, when Brian, Carl, Dennis, and Mike might sing some Everly Brothers, music was not a public affair. Usually, like teenagers all over L.A., they'd be cruising in somebody's beat-up junker, looking for girls and a good song on the radio. Kids, just plain kids, with no grand design and plenty of time. Up in the morning and off to class: Brian was the center fielder on the baseball team and the quarterback for the Hawthorne High Cougars. Tall and lean, he scrambles back, finds

a receiver, and throws a high spiral to Al Jardine, who drops the ball and breaks his leg in the ensuing pileup. The failed playmakers became fast friends, and although he wasn't even looking for it, Brian had found his fifth "Freshmen."

As Nixon debated Kennedy, the kids who would be Beach Boys were busy doing nothing. Brian had entered college at El Cerrito and was taking courses in music and psychology, although he continued to learn more from a three-minute record than he ever did in school. But if Brian fantasized about a life in music, that was between Brian and his four walls. Al Jardine had also entered college, eying a career in dentistry. Mike was married to his cheerleader girl-friend, who was pregnant, and held down two jobs: sheet-metal apprentice and gas station attendant. Dennis and Carl were kicking and clawing their way through high school (Carl, of all people, was a disciplinary problem). They had few dreams and no special prospects for the future. It was left to Al to provide a spark: he invited Brian and another friend to accompany him on an audition he'd wrangled with Murry's song publisher, Guild Music. They tried to sing like the Kingston Trio and the Four Freshmen, but Guild had no interest in a kid "copy" band with no original songs. Brian couldn't help but be piqued: in his imagination, where he could hear all his harmonies, Brian had been build-ing a better Four Freshmen, one that spoke more directly to the kids hanging out of their cars down at Foster's. When he taught the guys what he heard, and they all sang, he sensed the beginning of a sound, but it was a sound in search of a subject.

Dennis was a surfer, and with his sun-bleached hair and hot-dog patter he let everybody know it. Early in the morning he'd be starting out, catching the breakers, the hot sun, and the girls at the beach. At night Dennis'd talk about pipelines and wipeouts and rag on Brian to write a song about surfing. Brian, who was afraid of the water, gave Dennis the benefit of the doubt; after all, Dennis was a child of nature. "Across the U.S.A.," thought Brian, or at least

Dennis, the "physical" Beach Boy, was emotionally suited to pound out the big beat. But by the time of "Little Deuce Coupe" most of the studio percussion was handled by Hal Blaine, considered by many (including Phil Spector) to be the best session drummer in L.A.

The Beach Boys play a fraternity party at UCLA in the summer of 1962, the last days of the Twist, although Brian (third from right) appears to be doing the Monster Mash. David Marks is second from right. When Al returned to the group and David got the boot, he started a group called David and the Marksmen.

FACING PAGE:

KFWB deejay Roger Christian (right) got off the air at midnight and would meet Brian, who lived in Hollywood, to eat hot-fudge sundaes and write songs about cars.

across the South Bay, "everybody'd be surfing." Wouldn't that be nice? He and Mike wrote "Surfin'"—"Surfin' is the only life, the only way for me"—and Brian caught a hint of the music that he'd been singing in his room, and it didn't sound stupid or inadequate. It was his own sound—and Brian could feel himself about to smile, because it was good. When Murry and Audree took a trip to Mexico City and left the boys money for their care and feeding, they went straight down to the music store and picked out beefier instruments with which to get the beat really humming. The boys went and played the song for Hite and Dorinda Morgan at Guild Music, who agreed that they were onto something, arranged for studio time, and shopped around the resulting single (the B-side, "Luau," was a trifle written by the Morgans' son). A deal was struck with the Candix label, which issued it first on its "X" subsidiary and then on the parent label. But before a record could be pressed, the group needed a name. Daydream chatter had explored various possibilities—Carl and the Passions was one and Brian had previously credited a song recorded with Audree to Kenny and the Cadets. But at the time of "Surfin'," the guys pretty much agreed to name themselves the Pendletons, after their favorite shirt. The label had another idea—the Surfers—and later came up with its generic equivalent: the Beach Boys. Nobody was thrilled, but then nobody could deny that it fit a quintet of California kids who sang in harmony to a fast beat and who, more than likely, would come and go with the tide.

The Beach Boys

DENNIS   DAVE   CARL   BRIAN   MIKE

Once Murry had inked a deal with the big boys at the Capitol Tower, things were never the same around the Wilson household. Brian's hobby had become the family's vocation, and Hawthorne had come to Hollywood. Murry acted as manager, Audree kept the books, and Capitol promoted them as America's teenagers. There was no middle ground for the Beach Boys—they went from high school to high stakes, and were transformed from anonymous kids to teenage celebrities.

O N A MILD AND SUNNY MORNING IN THE WINTER of 1962, Murry Wilson walked out the front door, climbed into his car, and took the rush-hour drive from Hawthorne to Hollywood for an appointment at the Capitol Tower. "Surf-in'" had gotten him in the door, but if today went like his meetings at the other major labels, he'd be hustled out soon after a perfunctory listen to a demo tape that included "Surf-in' Safari," "Surfer Girl," and "409." Stupid kid music, thought Murry in his heart of hearts, except for one thing—these were *his* stupid kids, and he was their manager. Today was different: by sun-down Capitol Records had given Murry six hundred dollars for the demos, and Dad came home a hero. The Beach Boys were Capitol recording artists, but lest we forget, the music industry of which they were now a part did not have the sophisticated marketing techniques it has today. Teenage records were a dis-crete part of the market, the profitable tail of a healthy dog, and that was fine with the industry's old guard. There was no video. There wasn't even much rock and roll—Elvis had been drafted and the wimpy teen idols had taken over. Soon Beatlemania and the postwar baby boom would make the tail wag the dog, but when slick young A&R man Nick Venet played Murry's tape to his older boss Voyle Gilmore, what the men heard was a teenage fad: surf music. Bright, bouncy, and fast. But just to be safe—after all, where's a kid supposed to surf in Wichita?—they pushed a car song, "409," as the single's A-side. The kids in Phoenix, natch, flipped their woodies over the B-side, "Surfin' Safari," and sent it toward number fourteen on the national charts. Capitol had a happy handle on two fads, cars and surfing, and suddenly wanted an album yesterday. The group, with Nick Venet producing, Murry advising, and Brian learning

fast, cut most of *Surfin' Safari* in one thirteen-hour session. Considering the pace of the next four years, that was about normal.

Brian Wilson wears a coat of many clichés, including that of being "a man before his time." In the era of Brill Building songwriters, when faceless professionals turned out material for teen artists groomed by adults, he was composing songs for his own self-contained group, and within six months would be producing their records. Brian, the reticent kid from Hawthorne, had won creative control before there were even rock stars to demand it. Capitol was less than pleased when Brian moved the group from the corporate studios to Western Recorders because he liked the echo better, but as long as there was product—*lots* of product—they were willing to let him run wild.

Today a major group releases one album a year, tops, and through sophisticated marketing a hit LP can enjoy a lengthy shelf life. In 1962, if an album dropped on the charts, sales stopped cold, so companies pressed their artists to produce a constant flow of new material. From 1962 through 1966, with an average of three albums a year and a single every three months, Brian Wilson's productivity was unparalleled in popular music. Other groups maintained equally hectic recording schedules, but the songwriting and production duties were always shared. John had Paul, Paul had John, and they both had producer George Martin. Phil Spector had a coterie of musicians and singers to realize his vision. But, surrounded by the Beach Boys, Brian was basically a one-man show. In just three years, between 1963 and 1965, Brian led the group through *ten* albums. Filler was a necessary evil—timid surf instrumentals in the beginning, impossibly sophomoric shtick comedy later, and finally a more mature selection of cover songs. (Capitol rereleases of these albums acknowledge their haphazard programming by retitling the LPs after their biggest hit and deleting the utter dogs.)

The rigorous recording pace of the Beach Boys puts a necessary wrinkle in

Brian knew exactly what he wanted in the studio,
and while he'd always listen to the suggestions of
his group (especially Carl) and the supplementary
musicians, the end product would invariably match
what Brian had first heard in his head.

The Beach Boys would pose next to anything with wheels. Here Mike cops a couple of Z's (note the Beatles boots worn by him and Carl) and Glen Campbell plays the part of Brian.

critiquing the early work of Brian Wilson. When the group began, hit singles were the name of the game and albums surrounded these with filler. Brian produced hit songs aplenty and, as the years went by, wrote album tracks that could compete. But in aesthetic retrospect, we are left with many great songs and few great albums. Capitol merchandised the Beach Boys every which way, from putting all the car songs under one hood *(Little Deuce Coupe)*, to plugging a few others into *Shut Down,* a collection of "hot rod swingers" by various artists, including Robert Mitchum singing his bootlegger ballad, "Thunder Road." (By the time Capitol got around to releasing a Beach Boys album named *Shut Down,* they had to add a "Vol. 2.") The group's ninth LP, *The Beach Boys Today!,* released in March 1965, is considered by many to be the first thoroughly satisfying Beach Boys album: consistently tuneful and produced with an unprecedented (short of Phil Spector) attention to detail, it was wholly original and accurately pegged the Beach Boys, the U.S.A.'s most successful band, as the essential American link between the rock of the fifties and this brave new British world of the sixties. Later that year the Beatles would release *Rubber Soul,* the record that got the credit for establishing the album as the new state of the art. Brian dug the trend, as well as *Rubber Soul,* and set out to make an LP that was good from beginning to end, like one long single. One year (and two more LPs) later, the Beach Boys released *Pet Sounds,* Brian's "Fifth Symphony" and an enduring pop masterpiece. But no sooner had Brian learned how to make superb albums than the singles stopped becoming hits.

The early albums of the Beach Boys, which to this day dominate the core repertoire of America's longest-running rock band, offer clear signposts to Brian's quicksilver development. Through their third album, *Surfer Girl,* Brian's first production, the instrumentation was rudimentary and the lyrics revolved around the South Bay scene that they called home. Their sound was suburban white rock 'n' roll doo-wop, with nascent hints of musical sophisti-

Mike in Manhattan: For the Beach Boys, mass
transportation meant lots of kids in a car.

The Beach Boys contributed a number of ''swinging
song hits'' to beach movies, a B-movie genre that
was the cinematic equivalent to the Beach Boys'
songs of lowercase fun but nowhere near as lasting.
In this context, adults fit in about as comfortably as a
surfboard in St. Louis.

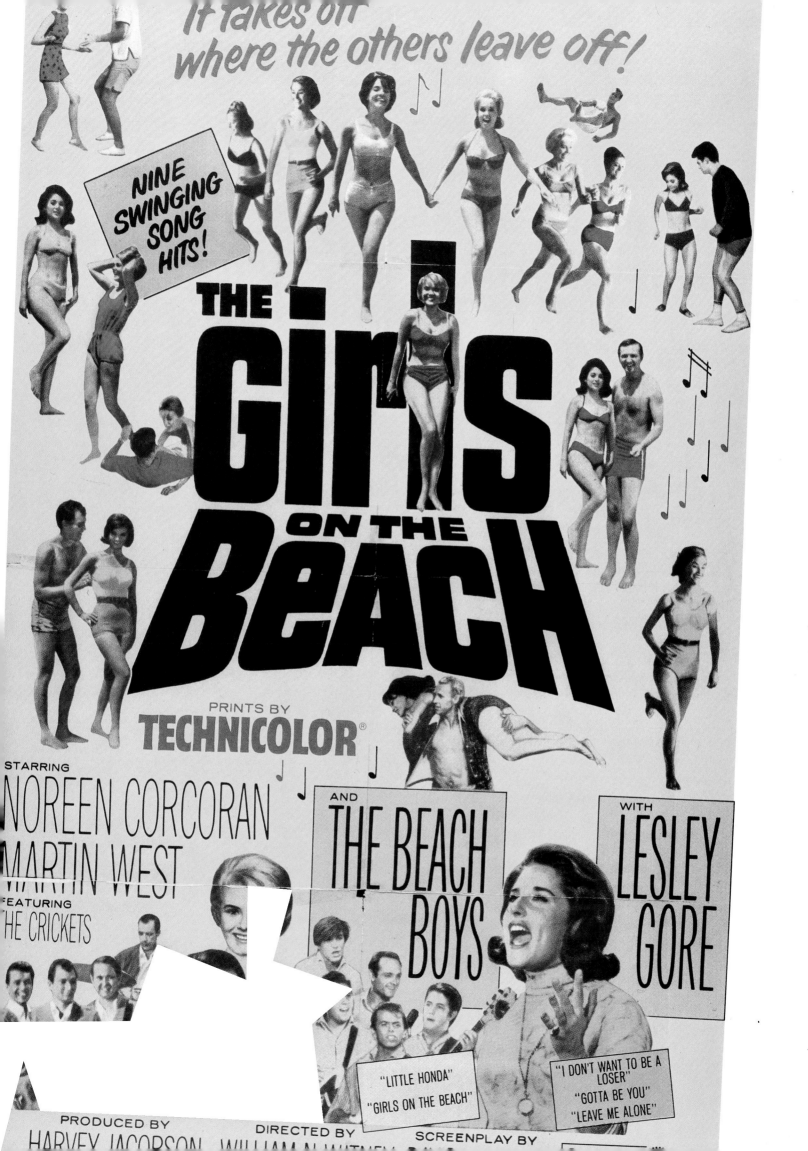

cation, particularly on the twin-peak ballads "Surfer Girl" and "In My Room," with the group singing arch but exquisitely rendered harmonies and Brian actively stretching his compositional vocabulary. On *Little Deuce Coupe*, Brian hot-waxed his first real hard rock production, with a series of buzzing beats that befit an album about hot cars and being true to your school. There was new spit to the instruments, now handled largely by professionals who also worked for Spector, and above it all, more than ever, was harmony. The Beach Boys, a band of voices, were gassed up and ready to roll, and between *Shut Down, Vol. 2* and *Summer Days (and Summer Nights)* they had the hammer to the floor. Brian's skill at production and arrangement was maturing at a heady pace while the lyrics, many by Mike Love, broadened their frame of reference to embrace summertime itself. By 1966, with *Pet Sounds,* "Good Vibrations," and an album that was going to be called *Smile,* Brian Wilson had led his group to the heady pinnacle of pop: art.

If individual Beach Boys albums were inconsistent, taken together to supply the music for one big platter party, the house would be bitchin' till the break of day. Beach Boys songs can be roughly divided into two categories—fun and girls—with appropriate subdivisions. For instance, the group's early fun songs can be divided between surf ("Surfin' U.S.A.," "Catch a Wave") and cars ("Shut Down," "Little Deuce Coup"). This sort of "fun" however, which was directly drawn from the California experience, is not to be confused with that found in songs of uppercase "Fun," most particularly "Fun, Fun, Fun" and "I Get Around." These tunes took a more generic if not monumental look at teenage kicks, and boldly stated that the search for good times was not just a necessary pursuit but a noble one as well. Girls, of course, were a given, they hoped, they prayed. On "California Girls" the world was one big dance card. But Brian's datebook was also filled with sweet songs of the joys and jagged edges of young love (from "Surfer Girl" to the entirety of *Pet Sounds).* Were the Beach Boys sexist pigs? Sexist, yes; pigs, no. In the early sixties in Hawthorne, the Beach Boys were simply boys.

The songs of the Beach Boys have survived more than two decades of accumulated cool because they were created in innocence. This is in part because the Beach Boys had a problem with hip. They weren't. Take Al: when the group was signing with Capitol, he weighed the pros and cons and decided to stick with dentistry. For a year a neighbor of the Wilsons', David Marks, played the truly existential role of the man who would be Al Jardine. Al came to his senses, of course, but an image was struck that was not exactly wild and rebellious. Their conservatism also showed in their clothes, from the candy-striped red-and-white shirts that became their visual albatross to the flammable acrylic V necks they sported on the cover of *Today*. These were sweaters only a mother could love—and that only she could make you wear. The Beatles, along with their darker counterparts the Rolling Stones, brought fab and groovy styles to rock and roll, as well as a notion that attitude was an essential part of the game. The Beatles were happy-go-lucky naturals, with smiles and sex and a certain *Je ne sais quoi*. Brian might have been the American genius of his musical generation, but the Beach Boys were about as sexy as a soft drink. They were like a clique of kids in everybody's tenth-grade homeroom—boyish but not handsome, funny but too sophomoric, talents but not artists. If Elvis was the King and the Beatles were exotic royalty, the Beach Boys were, well, like everybody else.

Precisely, except that hip, unlike innocence, is transitory, and the group sang like sandy angels. The Beach Boys were madrigal singers for an American age of limitless growth. Cash, cars, and five-part harmonies. They captured an America of sunlight and bright colors, and along the way Brian left Madison Avenue admen with a lexicon of melodies that suggest youthful American fun. This was a picture of America built with dreams and mirrors—life as one long

weekend—and in its frenzy to reap all the benefits of this Great Society, the country saw right through it and said yes. The Beach Boys, as cool as a cold Coke, created rock and roll by and for the American middle class. And America embraced the Beach Boys because when they sang, it was possible to imagine the fun going on forever.

If everybody had an ocean, across the U.S.A.
Then everybody'd be surfin', like Californiyah!

"SURFIN' U.S.A."

Capitol released the Beach Boys' first album, *Surfin' Safari,* in December 1962; within a year the group would have four albums. The LPs were scarcely over twenty minutes each, supershort by contemporary standards, but thirty-eight tracks by anybody, let alone some green kids, is quite a workload. For the first two albums Venet served as producer, with Murry looking over his shoulder and talking loud and Brian chipping in more and more of his own ideas. By the third album, *Surfer Girl,* Brian was the sole producer, his biggest milestone in a year of feverish creative growth. Recording artists, especially teenagers, did not direct their own repertoire and production. It took older, more experienced ears to understand the faddish teenage market. Brian broke this adage by simply chronicling his South Bay experience—or at least what he would have liked it to be. Like everybody who's been to high school, Brian knew that it was important to be cool and that the coolest guys had the right look and were on top of everything that was new. White Levi peglegs, Pendleton shirts, sneakers or, better still, bare feet—this was the early sixties look of the Beach Boys from Hawthorne. Cool guys had a gift for gab and were able to chop another kid without drawing too much blood, just to show who was boss. Surfing was cool, and with "Let's Go Trippin'" a twangy electric guitarist named

---

Dennis and Audree: Although Dennis was at odds with his father as a child, his mother says that her middle son was the most like her husband. In spite of the fact that he inspired the writing of "Surfin'," Dennis was not part of the original group. Audree insisted that he be included.

Dick Dale had already created an instrumental style of rock and roll that sounded kind of like shooting the curl. The Ventures made the sound nation-wide with songs like "Walk—Don't Run" and "Diamond Head," and an L.A. duo named Jan and Dean had hit with a vocal style of California pop that was white, bright, and cool. On the early Beach Boys albums, Brian put all of this together to create vocal surf music.

Brian has consistently cited the Four Freshmen as his primary early influence, and it's significant that he was attuned to the squeaky-clean style of jazzy white doo-wop rather than to the inner-city street-corner variety. Brian sought clarity in the voices, pure timbres that didn't fray at the edges. Mike was more into hitting the blue notes found in rhythm and blues, and his grittier influences gave the group a tougher bottom. But Carl, who had been playing the guitar since twelve, had what proved to be the key early influence—an infatuation with Chuck Berry's style of rock and roll guitar. The crisp claps of guitar that begin "Surfin' U.S.A.," the first single from their second album, rang a bell that wiped out everything that had come before. Where Brian had been driving a musical beach buggy, he was now racing with a powerful engine.

Traffic statistics confirm that the majority of baby boom drivers instinctively accelerate when either "Fun, Fun, Fun" or "I Get Around" comes on the car radio. These songs that were soon to spring from Brian's pen were celebrations of good old American car lust, born to burn rubber. Chuck Berry also knew about "motorvating" over the hill; the drivers in his songs had "no particular place to go," but you wouldn't expect them to cruise alongside the Beach Boys. No, when you live next to the ocean, your cars are woodies and they're pointed toward the beach and stacked high with surfboards. Maybe you drive by the hamburger stand looking for girls—some of them keep their boyfriends warm

PRECEDING SPREAD:

And then there were six: Capitol publicity photos most often pictured the touring group without Brian. Here's the whole group, with Bruce Johnston at dead center. Before joining the Beach Boys, Bruce and Terry Melcher (under the name Bruce and Terry) released such Beach Boy knockoffs as "Summer Means Fun."

at night, you know? Or maybe you just drive. The Beach Boys counseled that the American search for good clean fun began behind the wheel of a car.

"Surfin' U.S.A." hot-wired the guitar introduction to Berry's "Brown-Eyed Handsome Man" to the melody of his "Sweet Little Sixteen." (Early pressings of the song failed to credit Berry, an unfortunate and potentially litigious reflection of an era when white artists openly exploited black sources; Berry was subsequently given sole credit.) But Berry's influence on the early Beach Boys went beyond supplying a couple of guitar figures and one key melody—his best songs had shown how terse bursts of Americana could be strung onto a driving beat. More than any of the early rock and roll writers, he put the American vernacular into the music; professional tunesmiths like Leiber and Stoller were equally adept at turning words on a count of four, but compared to Berry's imaginative elocution, their world view was strictly Broadway. For Berry, "School Day" ("Ring, ring, goes the bell") was a matter of "Living in the U.S.A." ("everything you want they got it right here in the U.S.A."): his gift was in weaving a sense of the everyday into songs built to last. Berry was a poet of the American highways, but he was no Woody Guthrie: he was a rock and roller in the same boom time as the Beach Boys. Though peaking earlier, he was still of a time when the mass media, including an entertainment called rock and roll, was giving America a clearly defined national culture. California constituted part of Berry's American Dream—he called it "The Promised Land"—but Chuck left it for Brian to sketch out the particulars. Brian looked around him and beneath the sunny blue California sky he found a suburban landscape where images hang like oranges on the trees. Burgers and fries, Sting Rays and soda pop. With their first four albums, Brian Wilson and the Beach Boys became the pure pop poets of Summertime U.S.A.

Framed by Brian's music, the Beach Boys meticulously recorded the minutiae of the American Sun Belt and it was both boring and beautiful. The Beach

Boys have never been far from superficial. On the early records, where Brian was busy learning the techniques that would make him a seminal producer of sophisticated rock and roll, they worked their obvious words in obvious ways. It's no accident that the earliest songs we remember are the fad-oriented hit singles: "Surfin' Safari" and "409" from the first album, and "Surfin' U.S.A." and "Shut Down" from the second. From the outset, the Beach Boys have celebrated the inconsequential, the trivial pursuits, the things only a kid could understand. Brian sold fun, and it was the key that allowed him to take his music out of his room and into the world. The Beach Boys accepted fun as the price of success and had no worries—Brian could be as funny as the next guy.

The first four Beach Boys albums are luxuriously lightweight totems of their time. Surfin', cars, girls—these were the stocks and bonds of the teenage good life, and with the twilight exception of "In My Room," the group rarely dug deeper. With "Surfin' U.S.A." Brian had jumped his own gun and had shown how the luckiest kids in Hawthorne were going to alchemize the endless summers of Southern California into an all-American myth of eternal good times. He welcomed a kid from Sioux City, Iowa, to "Surf City" (a number one hit Brian wrote for Jan and Dean). Here there are "two girls for every boy," no parents, and fun, fun, fun. With the sand that passed through their toes, and our toes too, the Beach Boys built the kind of castles that are washed out to sea but never really go away.

Sittin' in my car outside your house,
Remember when you spilled Coke all over your blouse?
T-shirts, cut-offs, and a pair of thongs,
Oh, we've been havin' fun all summer long.

"ALL SUMMER LONG"

ABOVE:

Fun, Fun, Fun: Dressed like bankers, the Beach Boys
are suitably disguised to fool a young girl's father.

OVERLEAF:

Mike and Brian didn't always see things eye to eye.
Where Brian's artistic drive made him thrive on
experimentation, Mike's commercial instincts were
less inclined to rock the boat. Through the early
years, Brian got Mike to see things his way.

WENDY

Fm

,—
WEN

By
BRIAN WILSON

DY,   what   went   wrong?___

N NOVEMBER 21, 1963, BRIAN WAS OVER AT Mike's house, working on a melody that was kind of like "Surfer Girl" only sadder. Grappling for lyrics, Mike kept running flat into the opposite of fun: sad. "What good is the dawn," he wrote, "that grows into day? The sunset at night or living this way?" They went to sleep with a new kind of Beach Boys song— "The Warmth of the Sun"—and woke up to the news that President Kennedy had been shot. Camelot had been canceled, the British were invading, and for three years of brightly lit Technicolor the songs of Brian Wilson and the Beach Boys became rich and juicy slices of American folklore.

There was an epic scope to Brian's new songs that looked beyond summer to September. This is America 1964, and with space shots and assassins' bullets ringing in a new future, the Beach Boys aggressively celebrated a pleasurable present. Brian was no longer simply precocious in the studio, he was starting to define the art. His arrangements sprouted wings—woodwinds here, strings there, and harmonies everywhere. The sound remained remarkably simple— these were songs to sing along with—while becoming increasingly rich. "I'm gettin' bugged driving up and down the same old strip. I gotta find a new place where the kids are hip." We want fun, said these songs, lots of it, and we want it now. In the next three years, Brian would write and record "Fun, Fun, Fun," "I Get Around," "When I Grow Up," "Help Me Rhonda," "California Girls," "Barbara Ann," "Sloop John B.," "Caroline, No," and "Good Vibrations." Between singles, the Beach Boys would also release eight albums.

"Yeah, yeah, yeah" to the Beatles was "fun, fun, fun" to the Beach Boys— monosyllabic crucibles that offered detractors a ready put-down. But with

---

What with writing the songs, producing the records, and touring with the group, Brian was one busy guy. Where the other guys would break when the tour was over, Capitol would be after Brian for the next single.

From ''Shindig'' (pictured), to ''Hullabaloo,'' to
''American Bandstand'': during the mid-sixties the
Beach Boys were TV perennials.

uppercase "Fun, Fun, Fun," the Beach Boys tested the cynics' mettle with a souped-up Berry beat, a highway full of harmonies, and a lyric evoking the crime, punishment, and redemption of teenage kicks. "Well, she got her daddy's car and she cruised thru the hamburger stand now. Seems she forgot all about the library like she told her old man now." Radio blasting, she's off and speeding until her daddy takes the T-Bird away and she's left to find fun in the passenger seat of a boy's car. Contrasting the aimless freedom of cruising with the cutthroat parental threat of "grounding," "Fun, Fun, Fun" painted the teen's pursuit of pleasure as a grand and noble struggle. Here was life, here was bliss—two guys for every girl and a highway that led from one good time to the next. As on most of the fast songs, Mike's nasal voice took the lead while Brian's falsetto supplied the emotional counterpoint. The result: beach blanket doo-wop.

By early 1964, when the Beatles crossed the ocean to debut on "The Ed Sullivan Show," the Beach Boys were America's premier hitmakers. In the three years since Dennis suggested that Brian write a song about surfin', they'd ridden a long pipeline of Top Ten hits and had moved practice sessions from the Wilsons' music room to concert stages across the country. The Beach Boys escaped at least one pop cliché: paying the proverbial dues. Brian's team went straight from high school varsity to the pop big leagues. The Beatles had scuffled around Liverpool and played the seedier side of Hamburg before manager Brian Epstein cleaned them up for public consumption. The Beach Boys enjoyed no such rite of passage. They went from Hawthorne to Hollywood, and Murry became their manager as well as their father.

All Summer Long, released at the height of Beatlemania, highlighted the warm weather images that had become the Beach Boys' own, from the playtime lyrics of the title tune (used at the conclusion of George Lucas's *American Graffiti)* to the snapshots that served as cover art. Hondas, hot nights, and rock 'n' roll

---

Dennis's first vocal solo, "You're My Miss America"
on the *Surfin' Safari* album, revealed the influence of
Dion from, of all places, the Bronx. *Surfer Girl*
featured three Dennis vocals—"Catch A Wave,"
"Hawaii," and "Surfer's Rule."

hootenannies. "Ba-ba-ba, Ba-ba-bara Ann." America daydreamed over that album cover and imagined themselves sprawled along the Pacific, tan and brown, grilling hot dogs in the sand and running out for a pass thrown by Brian. If the film *Shampoo* captured the Southern California of the late sixties, *All Summer Long* caught the L.A. beach community at mid-decade.

"I Get Around," the leadoff anthem of *All Summer Long,* upped the adolescent ante of "Fun, Fun, Fun" by suggesting that sometimes there wasn't enough pleasure to be found in the old hometown. Sometimes you had to travel. "I get around," went the chorus, "from town to town. I'm a real cool head," sublime and assured, "I'm makin' real good bread." The group's finest fast song, "I Get Around," was a two-minute, fourteen-second joyride that set Mike's car-honk lead voice atop a hard rock vehicle supercharged with handclaps, twitching guitars, top-down harmonies, and a falsetto by Brian that came and went like a cool breeze. And yet for all its jocular postures, there was also an element of desperation in "I Get Around," as it suggested that fun was finite. The energy of youth, like the horsepower of a car, gave one the freedom to find a new place where the kids are hip. In a life construed as an endless summer, one couldn't afford to get old, because you had to run to keep from falling. It's like the chorus to "Little Honda," the album's ode to a "groovy little motor bike." As the lyric takes the novice through the first three gears, a background chorus sings "faster, faster" and, though the voices dissolve into a reassuring "it's all right," it is also quite clear that the faster you go, the harder you might fall.

First and foremost, boys fall for girls, and the seed of sadness that is entwined in the music of the Beach Boys is planted in romance. Years later Brian would admit to getting red-faced upon hearing his youthful falsetto and, while he doesn't say as much, one might assume that his feeling of being "revealed" is most acute on the ballads. "Surfer Girl," of course, is the quintessential Beach Boys ballad, with spare instrumentation and voices that slip by like mist to

leave the indelible picture of a lovely girl, alone and at the beach. Dew clings to this performance, both in the cool execution of the singing and in the wide-eyed affection that it expresses. "We could ride the surf together," sings Brian, swimming out into the wide-open world of first love, and though the song is rich with romantic potential, it is left unresolved as the singer boldly asks the object of his affections if she loves him too.

"Warmth of the Sun," which along with "Don't Worry Baby" was a pivotal song in defining the harmonic aesthetics of the Beach Boys, left our guy lost

When his breakdown gave him the excuse to quit the road, Brian devoted himself to expanding the style and execution of his songs. While he often verbalized his song arrangements to studio musicians, he was also adept at writing musical charts.

Stripes of a different color: mellowing out with an *a cappella* performance during a television appearance.

OVERLEAF:

The Beach Boys rock out: when things got hot, Brian would begin to bounce.

and lonely on that beach, with the surfer girl good and gone. Its introduction is one of the most achingly beautiful in rock, with Brian's pearly pure voice soaring out of the vocal bed with shy bravado and dancing about the lower notes as if hesitant to plant his feet. There's a cinematic sweep to this music and a crucial ambiguity to its lyrics that lifted it from beach blanket brilliance into the realm of enduring romantic pop. "The Warmth of the Sun" was Brian Wilson's first "standard"—a song that owed its strength not to the simple verve of the music or the sociological details of the lyric, but to an enduring mythos sketched in words and preserved in the emotionalism of the music. Spring— the rebirth of the warmth of the sun—is the same in Kansas as California, as is the troubled blush a lonely lover feels upon rediscovering the beauty of a solitary sunset. The world, the song says with the rich weave of its harmonies and the lonely melancholy of its solo voice, is a stage equally adaptable to triumph and tragedy. Circumstances come and go, but the sun, the moon, and the stars remain, blinking like beacons and challenging the romantic to make one last grasp for grace.

"Don't Worry Baby" is arguably the Beach Boys' most perfectly realized song. A narrative of romantic yearning and emotional insecurity set upon the chassis of a drag-strip challenge, its thick tufts of woolen harmonies produced an aesthetic statement of astonishing power. Lyrically pedestrian, the song achieved transcendence by using voices as if they were symphonic instruments. Brian structured his group's five voices as before—Mike holding down the bottom; Carl, Dennis and Al intermingling like a deep school of fish in the middle; and his own falsetto, as sweet as the cream in cappuccino, on top. The Beach Boys had always meant singing, but never before had the harmonies been so much at the center of the production. The icing on the cake here became the devil's food itself, a fact made most clear at the instrumental break, where a muffled guitar chord bumps against an insistent boogie piano until, in a rush

The Beach Boys never met a fad they couldn't put in 4/4 time. As soon as people pegged them as a surf group, they became hot rodders.

of emotional release, a tide of voices propels Brian's lead voice, perched on the curl of a wave, into the final verse. With its nuts-and-bolts construction, the song put its emotional weight on voices that are as slick and warm as the oil-stained pavement of the fast lane. Much is rightfully made of Brian's studio innovations, but his most potent magic was in finding perfectly simple solutions. Five voices, like the instruments in an orchestra or the shades on a palette of paint—these were Brian's primary colors.

Color Brian blue. Girls are the happy center of the Beach Boys' universe, but more often than not, the guy singing the song is alone and aloof, admiring the surfer girl as if she were from some other planet. The guy in these songs—Brian—reprised the "Surfer Girl" melody as the theme to *Girls on the Beach*, one of a raft of beach movies (many starring that ubiquitous beach bunny Annette Funicello) that depicted a Technicolor teen world of lowercase fun. A beach party would most likely give the guy in Brian's songs the willies, because who could know when you'd run into a broken heart—and it might not even be your own. On "Hushabye," one of a number of romantically blue doo-wop beauties that the group covered on their early albums, our boy vainly tries to brush away his girlfriend's tears. Somebody's usually unhappy in these songs of love, caught thinking about how nice it will be, or how good it was. These are sprung-tight virgins who have just recently learned that love hurts as well as heals. And in the life of every boy, beach or no, there is a girl like "Wendy," that idyllically innocent first love that the Beach Boys rendered in a minor masterpiece wherein multiple voices lay consoling hands on her jilted boyfriend crying from within his own inescapable loneliness. The dulcet wonder of "Wendy" is captured in its structure, with Brian's falsetto atop a vocal waterfall that drops to a sympathetic "oooo" as an unmannered Mike tells the story of a romance gone goodbye. "I can't picture you with him," he sings with boyish defensiveness, "his future looks awful dim," but our boy isn't about to punch out any headlights: he's a lover, not a fighter. And he's also somehow broken, because he knows not only that Wendy will find somebody new—Wendys always do—but that she'll never let him say goodbye.

The Labor Day coda to *All Summer Long* was "Don't Back Down," the last Beach Boys tune to innocently lash itself to the lifestyle and terminology of cars and waves. "Gotta be nuts," swelled the falsetto chorus, "show 'em now who's got guts." The earliest copies of the album inadvertently listed the song as "Don't Break Down," and as Brian's ambitions collided with the creatively explosive atmosphere fostered by the British invasion, he would break down but not back down. For through it all he had the thrill of his music, and the sunflower was just about to take full bloom.

Singles, tours, albums; tours, albums, singles; albums, singles, tours. Life as a Beach Boy in 1964 was one lone interstate, and Brian didn't have the time to think about braking. "I was rundown mentally and emotionally," he recalled in 1966, "jumping on jets, one-night stands, also producing, writing, arranging, singing, planning, teaching." He'd also just married sixteen-year-old Marilyn Rovell—they'd met nearly two years earlier when the Beach Boys were playing L.A.'s Pandora's Box and Brian spilled hot chocolate on Marilyn—whom he had already recorded as part of a girl group called the Honeys. (Early Beach Boys marriages were kept from the fan magazines, though it's doubtful that many teenage girls cared.) The wedding was in part prompted by Brian's sudden fear that he would lose her to somebody else (Mike was a prime suspect). Regardless, they made a most un-Beach-Boys-like pair—a Jewish girl from Chicago and a white-bread boy from Hawthorne—and predictably, Murry didn't approve. But that wasn't the worst of Brian's problems with Dad: the Beach Boys had fired him as manager.

For Murry, too, the Beach Boys were a dream come true. As kids, in his house, at his knee, they had learned to sing, and Brian—especially Brian—had

OVERLEAF:

In glittery garb, the honkies from Hawthorne
instinctively begin to dance like the Temptations.

Mike breaks up as Brian tries to do the duck walk
like Carl's hero, Chuck Berry.

shown special promise. So when the teenage combo found themselves in the real world, Murry was the natural man in charge. He quickly sold ABLE Machinery and was going to make damn sure that his sons would get everything that he had been denied. Murry never really understood the depth of Brian's gift, but he sure knew where it had come from. "You see," recalled Murry in 1971, "a manager and a father can be pretty rough. The kids hate the teacher's trying to give them knowledge, you know? And till they're grown up and married, they don't realize how nice the teacher was to bang at them, you know, to bang their ears."

Murry let only Mike, the oldest, drink beer, and would fine the guys one hundred dollars for swearing. Once when Dennis mumbled a four-letter word into his onstage microphone, Murry yanked him off his drum stand and beat him like a child. Then there was the matter of women on the road—or lack thereof—and perhaps worst of all, Murry's continued meddling in the group's recorded sound. (One associate paraphrased Murry in the studio talking behind Brian's back: "He can't hear a thing—deaf in one ear . . . He'd be nobody if it weren't for me. I made him. He needs me. I'm really the great songwriter—Brian writes terrible songs.") The result was a great rock irony: the band that sang of rescuing that fair flower from her fuddy-duddy father was bugged by *their* old man. While on tour in Australia the Beach Boys, who were now actually men, took their first real step from home. "We felt that even though my father had his heart behind it," said Brian, "because of the situation between father and son, you just seem to go nowhere." Murry went home and, according to his wife, stayed in bed for five weeks. Soon enough—too soon—Brian would follow.

Three brothers and a cousin on a misty beach. When they grew up to be men, their world began to encompass themes that were more complicated than summer fun.

OVERLEAF:

The Beach Boys meet the British paparazzi (and look the other way).

A Beach Boys practice session. Mike dabbled with
the saxophone in the early days, but never
practiced. Onstage he stuck to the tambourine and,
later, the theremin.

TWO DAYS BEFORE CHRISTMAS, 1964, BRIAN HAD HIS first breakdown on a plane bound for Houston, Texas, the first stop of a two-week tour. "I just put my head down and wouldn't even look at anybody," said Brian. If he had opened his eyes, he would have seen 360 degrees of pressure: Capitol's insatiable demand for product; Murry's insistence that Brian continue to perform concerts with the group that he had created; his provider role in the career and comfort of his extended family; and his personal artistic need to top himself at every turn. Brian's one good ear rang from the sound of the amplifiers and he was afraid of losing his hearing for good. He retreated to his room—his troubled, overworked head—and even slammed his hotel room door on brother Carl. He flew home and, in response to a request sent ahead of his arrival, was met at the airport not by his wife, and certainly not by Murry, but by Audree. Mother and son went to the old house in Hawthorne, by now vacant, and Brian, newly married, opened his heart and cried all night.

As four Beach Boys finished the holiday tour, Brian used the respite of illness to change his life: he was quitting the road. When Brian made his announcement during the *Today* sessions, the band itself broke down, but big brother was adamant—it was more important for him to concentrate on writing and production, to keep the Beach Boys supplied with great new songs to sing. The group had remained competitive on the charts, but increasingly their buttoned-down California cool began to look suspiciously old-fashioned when compared to the exotic bands from England, especially the Beatles. "Both our names started with 'Bea,' and both on the same label," said Brian. "I thought that was very amusing." Not to mention threatening. By concentrating on the recorded

---

OVERLEAF:

Flushed with their British celebrity, Brian, Carl, Dennis, and Mike each bought themselves a Rolls-Royce. Here, Mike wonders what the Pacific Coast Highway will look like from the other side of the car.

repertoire, Brian meant to compete with the Brits on his own terms: song for song, and soon, album for album. What's more, by dropping out of the road show Brian unconsciously underscored the fact that the Beach Boys were and always will be a band more of song than personality.

Glen Campbell, Brian's first stand-in on the road, was soon replaced by Bruce Johnston, an L.A. musician and songwriter whose falsetto and sunny demeanor fit the group as comfortably as a hot dog does its bun. As younger brother Carl assumed the leadership role within the touring outfit ("Carl was born thirty," said his mom.), Brian stayed in L.A., writing songs and producing backing tracks with the studio musicians on whom he had come to rely as his compositions became increasingly complex. Although much is made of Brian's competitiveness with the Beatles, his artistic mettle was most challenged by Phil Spector, the first auteur of rock and roll studio production.

If Brian was a product of middle-class normalcy, Spector was an urban compulsive straight out of the melting pot. Born in the Bronx, Spector spent his teenage years in L.A., hustling from one music gig to the next, until finally he sat behind the board himself. He built a wall of sound, or as he described it, "a Wagnerian approach to rock and roll: little symphonies for the kids." His songs pulsated with multiples of everything—guitars, drums, castanets, a thousand clapping hands—and leapt out of the car radio to hit you like a kiss. These were tough songs, street songs sung by groups like the Crystals ("He's a Rebel") and the Ronettes ("Be My Baby"). On the jukebox at his house, Brian would repeatedly blast the "da doo ron ron" out of Spector's great Philles' singles and marvel over their hard rock candy mountain. Spector and Wilson toed a similar stylistic line, with one crucial difference: where Phil had his girl groups, Brian sang with a group of guys.

During the dizzy days of *Smile*, Brian put up a tent inside his house. The ventilation was nonexistent, and he rarely went inside. Atop the pyramid is Brian's beagle Banana, one of the cameo stars on *Pet Sounds*.

OVERLEAF:

Traveling Men: "I've been all 'round this great big world, and I've seen all kinds of girls."

The Beach Boys Today!, released in March 1965, bore the first fruits of Brian's stay-at-home strategy, and the promotional line on its back cover—"A program of big Beach Boy favorites ... plus some great new Brian Wilson songs"— spelled out a future split between the group's commerciality and Brian's artistry. Working with a cadre of polished studio pros, Brian built his own wall of sound, although, given his penchant for harmonic voices, it was more accurately a wave. Brian and Phil were both looking for the same kind of sophisticated pop sound—Brian once called his songs "pocket symphonies"—but they were two different types of auteurs. Spector's work was indistinguishable from his personality—"Dig," said his songs, "this is the sound created by America's first teenage millionaire." Brian exerted the same autocratic control, but his productions, even a literal Spector copy like "Then I Kissed Her" (as in "Then I Kissed Him"), spoke through the personality of the group.

The sequencing of *Today* put the "Beach Boy favorites," the stuff that would go over like gangbusters in concert, on side one, thereby creating a full-blown California dance party, and the most masterfully sustained rock and roll production of Brian's career. Had Dick Clark, who blooped out the LP's obsequious liner notes, asked the teens at "Bandstand," they would have agreed that it had a good beat and that you could dance to it too. There was hardly a car in sight—now the Beach Boys signified fun by simply playing rock and roll. As for the "great new Brian Wilson songs," they were featured on a flip side of cool velvet make-out music, where Brian, without collaboration, spoke to the life of the heart, not the beach.

Bobby Freeman's "Do You Wanna Dance?" convened the first side with a rumbling rhythm track that thumped through the verse and held back for a second before joining a discothèque full of voices in a swoon of youthful exuberance. Closing the side, Brian's own "Dance, Dance, Dance" hooked the listener from beat one, with a descending bass riff joined by a rippling guitar and shaking bells that introduced an adenoidal Mike proclaiming a 3 P.M. call to arms: "After six hours of school I've had enough for the day, I hit the radio dial and turn it up all the way." The arrangement is a perfect exploitation of the Beach Boys' harmonies, with Carl, Al, and Dennis supplying a "dance, dance, dance" chorus, Brian pirouetting on top, and the voices merging at the end for an ascending final call to get on the good foot.

"Good to My Baby" and "Don't Hurt My Little Sister" are tuneful confections that similarly exploit harmonies, but the touchstone here is doo-wop. The introductions tell all: on "Good to My Baby," Mike's bass voice states the theme, is subsequently buttressed by an "ooooo" background, and is finally iced with Brian's falsetto; Brian keynotes the beginning of "Don't Hurt My Little Sister," leading the group in three statements of the chorus hook in descending keys. Though minor songs in the composer's canon, top-notch performances and Brian's keen ear for detail have allowed them to age with a remarkable freshness.

"When I Grow Up" was not only the most ambitious song on this party platter, rippling with harpsichord fills and featherbed harmonies, it also served to introduce the more mature mode of side two. On the one hand, it was adolescent and gawky ("Will I look for the same thing in a woman that I dig in a girl?"). On the other, that of a man-child artist creating in a world defined by teenage concerns, it rang all too true: "Will I dig the same things that turned me on as a kid? Will I look back and say that I wish I hadn't done what I did?" The sophistication of the arrangement, constructed so that it would continually circle back on itself, stood in sharp contrast to a background track in which the years of our young lives (but only as far as the age of thirty-two) are counted in unyielding succession.

"Please Let Me Wonder" opened the side of "great new Brian Wilson songs" with his subtlest wall of sound yet—the arrangement was full but airy, light

OVERLEAF:

Striped shirts gone, the Beach Boys pose as gothic hippies. From the very beginning, Brian blended voices in search of the spiritual "oooo."

as a summer romance but rich enough to do it justice. The vocal purr rekindled "Don't Worry Baby," but the giddy beat of bass and drum and a guitar that simply stroked one's spine evoked the wild heart of a boy kissing his first girl. Insecurity peeks through the sweetness of Brian's lead voice; as if wiped out by the mere possibility of having found true love, he's afraid to ask this particular Wendy for confirmation. This California teen isn't about to ask, "Did you come?" Rather, fearful that reality won't match his dreams, he's satisfied with rapturous wonder. Soothed and suckled by stylishly rendered latter-day doo-wop—"I'm So Young" and "Kiss Me Baby"—the listener is shaken to attention by "She Knows Me Too Well," wherein an aching melody rides atop a pinched drum beat that answers Brian's hesitation on "Please Let Me Wonder." Here his love is placed in the real world, where other guys are ready to steal your girl and one's own insecurities become not a matter of wistful convenience but dangers in themselves. But with the right woman, one who knows you too well, the shy romantic is successfully seduced into making his own declaration: "Yes," he says, opening up to the world, if still fearful of the consequences, "and I love her too."

Though relieved of his concert duties, Capitol's hunger for product continued to push Brian at a breakneck pace—three months after the release of *Today,* as if to commemorate the passing of the seasons, the Beach Boys released *Summer Days (and Summer Nights).* Carl cites it as his brother's first album-length production, but it was really a peculiar combination of quickie product and offhand brilliance. Capitol wanted a summer album; Brian was already warming up for *Pet Sounds.* But in early 1965, when Brian couldn't help but toss six TDs while recording an album, he could still fulfill his lifelong ambition to please everybody. He'd challenge himself with a production like "Salt Lake City," wherein Brian imagined Spector paying tribute to the home of the Mormon Tabernacle Choir, and please Capitol with junk like "Amusement Parks

U.S.A.," which doubled as the itinerary of your baby brother's dream vacation. Brian's best songs, however, addressed that kid's older sister.

"Girl Don't Tell Me," with a wound-up melody the Beatles could envy, found Brian exploiting the summer theme with lyrics that pulled a reverse see-you-in-September. "I'm the guy-hi-hi who left you with tears in his eyes," sings Carl, and for good reason, because the romance is a bust by Columbus Day. "Girl don't tell me you'll wri-hi-ite," he continues, rising three notes on the last word, and while you know he'll keep checking the mailbox, it's made clear that come next June, he will act upon this painful lesson. "But this ti-hi-ime I'm not going to count on you. I'll see you this summer but forget you once I get back to school." Increasingly, the guys in these songs are left outside of love, and on "Let Him Run Wild," a headlong rush of instruments and voices that spin through an interlocking series of times and keys, Brian encourages his latest crush to dump the heel she's with and come to somebody who'd love her true. The song crystallizes at its most strident moment—Brian seconding the chorus with a "let him run" in a surprisingly shrill falsetto—to reveal that the singer is the prince charming of whom he speaks. While the Rolling Stones, aggressive and vengeful, were singing "Under My Thumb," Brian was pledging to keep his girlfriend warm at night.

Everything on *Summer Days,* however, including the single version of "Help Me Rhonda," paled next to Brian's smash-hit masterstroke, "California Girls." For the man looking to construct "pocket symphonies," the introduction to this song found the concept within his grasp. Keyboards and guitars gently interlock on a chordal sequence punctuated by cymbal flourishes, and as it's repeated, a bed of horns enrichens the bottom until all the instruments well up toward a brief pause as if a pin were going to drop, or as it happens, a carnival organ were about to turn this suite into a rock and roll anthem. As the organ slips into a roller-rink rhythm and a sharp snare drum repeats the cymbal fill,

OVERLEAF:

The touring group awaits a lift to the next show.

Mike grabs the lead and sings what may be the greatest of all Beach Boy fantasies: that they could *all* be California girls. No romantic insecurity here, not to mention jaded Hollywood starlets—just a bevy of "the sweetest girls in the world." The song encouraged the whole country to appreciate their hometown women—"Well East coast girls are hip, I really dig those styles they wear. And the Northern girls, with the way they kiss, they keep their boyfriends warm at night."—but their California hearts inevitably returned to the state and the myth that they helped to create. No matter how those "Midwest farmers' daughters" make you feel, or the way those Southern girls talk, they just can't compare with Wendy, Rhonda, and all the other girls at the beach.

As time went by, the overt chauvinism of "California Girls" came to represent the retrogressive nature of the Beach Boys' world view. But as with many of their great tunes, such debate seems churlish next to the accomplishment of Brian's music, which is precisely why it has remained a standard through decades of feminist ferment. Of course it looks upon women like precious tokens of style over substance; what is significant is that there's nary a hint of malice in "California Girls." This is boastful mythmaking by all of the romantic losers—the guy burned by last summer's romance, the one caught wishing on Wendy, and the stranger spying on the surfer girl. And as the closing harmonies build into waves of cresting counterpoints, buffeting and blissful, the Beach Boys graciously celebrate the better half of their California dream. The giddy grandeur of "California Girls" transcends sexual politics to imagine the romantic potential that all those girls offer all those boys.

The adventurous work of *Today* and *Summer Days,* culminating in the single success of "California Girls," his most sophisticated arrangement to date, emboldened Brian to take the step toward making an album as good as its best song. Still, as he planned and composed fragments of music Capitol was already waiting for a new album, especially as their follow-up single, "The Little Girl

I Once Knew," stalled as dramatically as its four-beat rest. A live album was out of the question—Capitol had released one the previous year—so while playing volleyball, Brian came up with an equally efficient way to create instant product: *Beach Boys Party!* Ostensibly this LP put you, the listener, smack dab in the middle of a swinging hootenanny, Beach Boy style, although most of the album was actually recorded in loose studio sessions with the tape rolling. *Party* was the musical equivalent of their excruciating attempts at cutup comedy, but it was much more fun to hear them goofing on Dylan, the Beatles, and themselves than talking about how good the bread is in France or how Mike's nose sounds as if it's on the critical list. What's more, by putting the increasingly self-conscious rock form into a rumpus room atmosphere, *Party* demystified the process and made a clear statement that pop music should first and foremost be fun. And when Dean Torrence (of Jan and Dean) wandered into a studio session, popped open a bottle of Coke, and suggested that they try "Barbara Ann," the revelers grabbed a hold of the "Ba-ba-ba, Ba-ba-bara Ann" chorus like a burger fresh off the grill. On the eve of their most sophisticated work, and with Brian already packing away his teenage tokens, the Beach Boys hit with one of the simplest songs of their career. "Barbara Ann" went Top 10 with a smile. It would never again seem so simple.

Could I ever find in you again,
Things that made me love you so much then?
Could we ever bring them back
Once they have gone?
Oh, Caroline, no.

"CAROLINE, NO"

OVERLEAF:

Brian is of two minds about acid: "I learned a lot of things, like patience, understanding"; "LSD shattered my mind."

WITHOUT SAYING GOODBYE, WITHOUT even knowing it, Brian had left the Beach Boys. They were out on the road, men performing his teen dreams, and he was back at home, in his room, looking to become a man. On stage Brian had found acceptance for the bell-like falsetto that used to draw the taunts of schoolmates; on *Pet Sounds* it would be the central instrument in a pop opera about coming-of-age. This was not an album of sandy mementos and innocuous emotions, but a record of hushed maturity and adult artistry. The subtle, puzzle-box construction of Brian's new songs transcended the production's stylistic debt to Phil Spector, just as the personal nature of the lyrics went far beyond the postcard scenarios that had dominated previous Beach Boys lyrics. In fact, if not in literal execution, *Pet Sounds* was Brian's first and only solo album, the full realization of the growth that he had begun in earnest with "The Warmth of the Sun." *Pet Sounds,* which has endured as only the best art can, was also the beginning of the end of the Beach Boys' long day (and longer night) in the sun.

Brian and Marilyn, struggling through the early years of their marriage, had moved into a house in Beverly Hills, where Brian smoked hash, dabbled in LSD, and scored the sounds inside his head. ("I learned a lot of things," he said of acid in 1966, "like patience, understanding." "LSD," he told Mike Douglas

Mike's stage wardrobe reflected his involvement with Transcendental Meditation. His sophomoric stage patter, however, remained the same. "There's one thing I do that's kind of a personal thing," he's said. "I tell jokes sometimes which are corny, which are outright stupid and bomb. That, to me, is funny when nobody laughs."

OVERLEAF:

Commencing with their British tour of 1966, the Beach Boys traveled with a larger ensemble that often included horns.

ten years later, "shattered my mind.") At twenty-three, he was belatedly struck by the emotional traumas that can come with so-called maturity. Brian's solution was to build a sandbox—2½ feet high with a truckload of sand—for the piano. Now he could compose at the beach without going anywhere near the ocean. The Beach Boys had gone from high school to high stakes, with Brian's songs giving them a fictitious adolescence that could be envied by any teen. That was the riddle of upper-case Fun: summer was never that good!—even if you're an upper-case Beach Boy. Innocence was still at the center of Brian's new songs, but increasingly, especially now that the singer might actually wake up with Wendy, a dark, restless fear was blended into the fun and girls. *Pet Sounds,* as deep and lovely as a wishing well, carries the echo of melancholy.

Music was never a problem for Brian—it was the means by which a guy who didn't have much to say expressed himself. Words were a problem. Although Brian had recently written more of his own lyrics, he had a consistent history of collaborators. Mike was the first—a partnership spawned from those nights singing along with the radio blasting—and would most often be the last. Gary Usher and Roger Christian, two Hollywood music and radio types, each wrote during the surf and hot-car days.

Collaborating with Brian was a lucrative, largely one-sided affair: Brian himself defined the song, if only by the powerful moods evoked by his music, and would work in his own words as well. But he was a musician first, and knew that the lyrics weren't keeping pace. He called Tony Asher, an advertising copywriter whom he'd met hanging around the studio, and asked him over to the house to talk about writing songs. (This is as if somebody called the proud owner of a little deuce coupe and said, "Hey, how'd you like to race at Daytona?") Brian played Asher an instrumental track of "Sloop John B.," a brilliantly arranged, smash-hit up-dating of a Kingston Trio song, and "In My Childhood," which ultimately evolved into the album's subtle evergreen, "You

Still Believe in Me." Asher, no dope, got a leave of absence and began a project wherein he'd generally write the first-draft lyrics, which Brian would polish and string within a score fit for pearls.

Pet Sounds, a dense underbrush of rhythm and melody, was recorded in a manner suited to its fragmentary composition. A full roster of musicians, often including horn and string sections, was called to Western Recorders where Brian, who could afford this expensive indulgence, would have a musical fragment, a piece of the puzzle, dancing in his head. That might be a chord progression or harmonic idea, and after teaching the players their parts, either by literal demonstration or verbal coaching, he'd cut the track, often mixing down a final dub as the musicians played. Returning home to work with Asher, they'd listen to acetates of the sessions and Brian would begin to pick out melodies on the keyboard. Soon the pieces would begin to fall into the big picture, and as Asher wrote the lyrics Brian would construct the completed instrumental track. (In 1968 the ever-resourceful Capitol released the instant collector's item *Stack O' Tracks,* featuring the instrumental backing to Beach Boys songs. Which is to say, Brian's music.) With his group out on the road, an impatient Brian would record the vocals by himself and later teach the layered harmonies to the Beach Boys. "He'd have four- and five-part chords in his mind," recalls Mike, "and he'd dish them out to all of us." Then, his ear tuned to the other four for mistakes, Brian would take the top part, the melody, and soar like a bird. Later, if he was dissatisfied with the group's vocals he'd return to the studio and recut them himself.

Brian's personal dealings weren't as meticulous as his music. Asher, for one, has described Brian as a genius musician but an amateur human being. The music making was a joy, he has said, whereas the social rigamarole that preceded each day's work was childish petulance. Van Dyke Parks, Brian's next lyricist, saw game playing in Brian's personal dealings, because by acting the

OVERLEAF:

Brian may be the most significant white pop artist least influenced by black music, but that doesn't mean he was averse to sole food. According to Derek Taylor, "a meal with him was like the Mad Hatter's tea party."

eccentric genius "he can always plead insanity." Brian was responsible to music because, unlike people, it had never let him down. When the music flowed Brian could get away with murder, because he was the artist, the creator, the man who baked the cake. And the music of *Pet Sounds* flowed like a deep river.

Pet Sounds is both the sound of Brian's dogs, Banana and Louie, chasing a train at album's end, and the songs themselves. Though not planned as an overtly conceptual LP, the song sequence created a lose narrative tracing a young man's lonesome journey toward maturity. Our young hero was once the spurned summer lover of "Girl Don't Tell Me," but as we join him he's already absorbed another measure of loss and disappointment. "Wouldn't It Be Nice" and "Caroline, No" bookend the LP and broadly sketch its themes as our boy goes from believing that grown-ups are lucky to losing the best thing he ever had. "Caroline, No," according to Bruce Johnston, "was directly about Brian himself and the death of a quality within him that was so vital. His innocence. He knows it, too."

"Wouldn't It Be Nice" begins our story with young lovers sneaking kisses in the living room and dreaming of an all-night future. "Maybe if we think and wish and hope and pray it might come true. Baby then there wouldn't be a single thing we couldn't do." Bright spring fantasies—sung by Mike through cupped hands as if leading a football cheer—this is first love, and the wood-winds yelp in happy approval. The elegiac ballad "You Still Believe In Me" introduces guilt, where our man-child discovers that vows whispered in private can be rescinded in public. A choral fade, stately and measured, lulls us into "That's Not Me," our first major plot point—the teen leaves home, and steps into the big bad city. "I could try to be big in the eyes of the world, but what matters to me is how I could be to just one giirrrl." Emotions swell as that last word is draped over a creamy cluster of chords, and Brian finds Spectorian drama in the heart of Hawthorne. "I once had a dream so I packed up and split for the city," he admits, anxious and a bit desperate. "I soon found out that my lonely life wasn't so pretty."

Throughout the album, one song is answered by the next: "Don't Talk (Put Your Head On My Shoulder)," with Brian's solo voice swaddled by a chamber group, comforts our road warrior within the arms of just one girl. "I'm Waiting For The Day" casts our characters in disturbing new roles: an affair where the woman is the left and lonely one, and the man is waiting for the day when she can love again. This is "Let Him Run Wild" only worse, because now it's clear that while you can leave a past love, it's likely to stubbornly sing-along with your future. "Let's Go Away For Awhile," the first of two movie-music instrumentals, swoons like seabirds flying out to meet the "Sloop John B.," included at Capitol's insistence. Though compatible with the completed work's lofty standards, the song would forever remain a stylish standout, a debutante at the wrong party.

"God Only Knows," the crown jewel of Brian's patchwork style of composition, opens side two. In its introduction a bass guitar knits together keyboards and french horns before gently receding into the first verse: "I may not always love you, but as long as there are stars above you, you'll never need to doubt it, I'll make you so sure about it." Brian initially anguished over using the word "God," fearing commercial repercussions, but the image fit together like bread and wine. Life is nothing without your love, says the singer, and while this is as old as the moon in June, its tie to the heavenly spirit opened a skyful of allusions. A rich tapestry sprinkled with golden thread, Brian's music celebrated the transcendent power of art. An instrumental bridge in the song, clearly one of those independently recorded "fragments," finds bass and strings orchestrated around a dogmatic drum flourish. A chorus appears, building voice upon voice, brick after brick, until the melody breaks like the dawn. The seamless integration of independent passages, the keynote of *Pet Sounds* and beautifully realized in "God Only Knows," was the work of a man at the peak of his creative powers. And when one reaches for the moon, the stars will often fall into line: during the fade of "You Still Believe In Me," a bicycle horn adds a charming snatch of homespun percussion. The technology of recording was still relatively unsophisticated in 1966—*Pet Sounds* was recorded, mostly live, on a four-track machine, an extraordinary achievement—and this early embellishment was locked into the best of the rhythm tracks. In the end Brian wanted to take it out, but that was impossible. Was it simple fate that left those childish honks to create their own special moment? God only knows, and he's not telling.

Yin and yang, love and loneliness. The switch-off continues on "I Know There's An Answer" (with lyrics by Terry Sachen), where, over a track thickened by horns, banjos, and a platoon of percussionists, our man is up and fighting. "I know there's an answer," says Brian, who has never strayed far from his family, "I know now, but I had to find out for myself." And one of the things he finds out is that girls can also break a promise. The woman of "Here Today" is not the sweet and innocent "Surfer Girl," because according to the singer, he's "the guy she left before you found her." Strung tight over an exhilarating sea of time changes and swirling instruments, the song pulls us gently, imperceptibly, out into deep water. "Love is here today," sing the boys, "and tomorrow it's gone."

Slowly, inexorably, these songs dig deeper and deeper still. The lover, like Brian himself, is left running in circles, alone, like everybody else, and looking for the same thing. "I've been trying hard to find the people that I won't leave behind," go the lyrics to "I Just Wasn't Made For These Times," Brian's most personal statement outside of "In My Room." This song is about a man lost in love, but it's also about art and life. A large, lonely ache pervades this performance, balanced delicately between the stately measure of the harpsichord and the rattle of the percussion. This is Brian courting his first and only love, music, and wondering who will accompany him. "Every time I get the inspiration to go change things around," sings the artist, the lover, the older brother, "no one wants to help me look for places where new things might be found." Sad, resigned, he restates the title: "I guess I just wasn't made for these times."

Nineteen sixty-six, and Brian puts the cap on youth and his first and final full-length production. The title-track instrumental, as comfy as blue jeans and a Pendleton shirt, lulls us toward the final denouement, "Caroline, No"—romance when innocence is gone, and music when your heart is broken. Drummer Hal Blaine—thunk—hits the bottom of a plastic bottle of mineral water—thunk—and contributes the most emotional piece of percussion in all of rock. "Where did your long hair go?" asks the boy who is now a man. "Where is the girl I used to know?" She's a stranger, and he's now in a strange land. He looks around him: it's nighttime and everything looks the same, but he knows it's different. He hears the dogs, Banana and Louie, out in the fields, running down a train. Tomorrow would come, as sure as that train, and the dogs would give chase, but from now on and forevermore there would be a cold chill amidst the warmth of the sun.

In merry old England, it was thumbs up for the boys
in the mid-sixties.

A dozen years down the line, the Beach Boys relive
the photo shoot for *Summer Days (and Summer
Nights)*. This time Al doesn't have the "flu bug."

OVERLEAF:

When Brian abandoned the studio, Carl became the
Beach Boy most likely to approximate his classic
sound. By 1971's "Feel Flows" and "The Trader,"
he would be recording himself as a one-man band.

WHOOSH—BRIAN WILSON ROLLS COOL and solemn through the Los Angeles night toward yet another recording session for what will become his enduring pocket symphony, "Good Vibrations." As in many an old Beach Boys song, the car is key: Brian rode in a Rolls-Royce that had once belonged to John Lennon. But Capitol wasn't about to confuse the Beach Boys with the Beatles—*Pet Sounds* had been a serious commercial stiff. Brian had produced the most sophisticated album in the history of rock and roll, technically and musically, and the public said that what they really wanted was *Party*. Brian was depressed—his records had never *not* sold, his family *did* depend on him, and he hated it when people, especially Murry, told him that they'd told him so. But he was also happy: *Pet Sounds* was one hell of a record. Capitol pulled the promotional plug almost immediately, rush-releasing *Best of the Beach Boys,* and for the first time—it wouldn't be the last—forcing the group to compete with their past. But *Pet Sounds* carried a silver echo—it broke the bank in England, and gave Brian the critical respect and hip credentials that he so deeply desired and deserved. National magazines called for interviews, and he was on the A-list of L.A.'s cool people. Sitting in the back of a luxury car fit for a Beatle, Brian could still afford to fool around and make art.

Al doodles at the piano in Brian's Bel Air home studio. Without a doubt, his most famous vocal was the lead to "Help Me Rhonda," which the Beach Boys cut twice. The uncharacteristically bloated version on *Today* is twenty-two seconds longer than the sprightly hit single released in May 1965 and included on *Summer Days (and Summer Nights)*.

Nineteen sixty-six, and if you squinted your eyes, and maybe smoked some Mexican pot, you could see the dawning of the Age of Aquarius. The pop explosion of the past few years had opened the doors for a bold new type of boho. No longer was bohemia an isolated group of lefties with a taste for cheap wine and poetry read over cool jazz; now it was a whole generation. Hippies were everywhere, even in Hawthorne, and aside from the commercial considerations that had already caused friction within the group, the true challenge for the Beach Boys was to decide whether they'd find a place in the future or safely ride out their past. Hippies were naturally skeptical. Rooted in family, and celebrants of a consumer society that the youth culture was busy both exploiting and rejecting, the Beach Boys carried the burden of proof. They had finally shucked the striped shirts, and their hair was crawling over their collars, but when push came to patchouli, could innocent fun really be considered relevant?

Rock and roll, if only by the sheer number of people relating on the same sounds, had become the touchstone of the emerging counterculture. Bob Dylan had revitalized the folk tradition, and when he shocked the purists by putting his poetry in front of an electric rock band had challenged rockers to say more than "yeah, yeah, yeah," if not "fun, fun, fun." Brian was both appreciative and inhibited by Dylan's wordplay; he worried that his concentration on verbal intensity was at the expense of the musical sophistication that Brian thought pop deserved. The Byrds were L.A.'s hip new harmony group, and while their folk rock vocal scores were less complex than Brian's, they were bona fide hippies, and that was important. Sophistication's a tough sell, particularly when everybody thinks of you as driving a woodie. Brian wasn't worried. In the back of John Lennon's Rolls—"Hey, how about stopping at Pioneer Chicken on Sunset Boulevard?"—Brian began to plan an album that would embrace a concept so unhip it hurt: God.

On magazine covers of the sixties, God was dead. Brian figured It lived in the spiritual "ooooo" sent up by the intermingling voices of the Beach Boys. "I'm writing a teenage symphony to God," he told this real erudite writer and player he'd met on producer Terry Melcher's lawn. Murry would have flipped; Mike would have had a cow. Van Dyke Parks, who looked rather elfin next to Brian, who was beginning to munch himself toward fat, just nodded his head. Brian was echoing his stylistic mentor, Phil Spector, but by now the crucial difference between the two was clear: Brian was not afraid to change, and loved to experiment. Spector had stalled, and after the U.S. failure of his 1966 self-proclaimed mega-single, Ike and Tina Turner's "River Deep, Mountain High," had gone into a retirement that was starting to generate paranoid stories of guns and locked mansions. Brian was no more tripped out than the rest of this hip new crowd he was hanging out with. In its earliest stages his religious LP was to be called *Dumb Angel,* but as work progressed and it became clear that the sophisticated purity and good cheer that Brian sought could actually be personified by the Beach Boys, it got a more poetic tag: *Smile.*

"Good Vibrations," originally written during the preparation of *Pet Sounds* and considered for inclusion therein, was perhaps Brian's most favorite sound. Aiming for avant-garde rhythm and blues, he was willing to try every kind of trick. One of them was a buzzy little instrument called the theremin that had debuted in the score of *Spellbound,* Alfred Hitchcock's 1945 Freudian shocker in which Salvador Dali designed Gregory Peck's dreams. The theremin fit right in, but "Good Vibrations" seemed to tease Brian and defy his capture. He cut a live version at Western studios, and everybody loved it but Brian. He stretched his method of fragmentary composition and execution to radical extremes: over six months, in four different studios, and on over ninety hours of tape, he proceeded to record over a dozen completed versions. His aim was to re-create the live version from separate but equally perfect individual pieces.

Dean Torrence was half of the singing surf duo Jan
and Dean, who had hits before the Beach Boys even
recorded, but never sounded better than when Brian
wrote them songs like "Surf City." Jan Berry
sustained severe brain damage during a near-fatal
car crash in 1966. At the right, Brian and Dean work
in the studio with Marilyn and her sister Diane
Rovell, who acted as music contractor during many
mid-sixties Beach Boys sessions.

Fifty thousand dollars in recording costs for one single record—Capitol thought he was nuts, and so did some of his band. It was too long, they said, and sure not "Help Me Rhonda." Brian said "No, it's not going to be too long a record, it's going to be just right." Finally, one night, Brian got the nod: "I remember I had it right in the sack. I could just feel it when I dubbed it down to mono. It was a rush—a feeling of" (and here one can sense the composer swallowing an inclination to blush) "artistic beauty." The term rock and roll is too specific to apply to "Good Vibrations"—better to call it extraordinary music that climbed the heights of innovation and peeked over the top. Or more simply, art. An engineer present at both the first and last session for "Good Vibrations" scratched his chin: Brian's in-the-pocket version of "Good Vibrations" sounded remarkably like the first night at Western.

Brian might have been a nerdy hippie, but he knew how to do his own thing: "Good Vibrations," released in October of 1966, leaped out of the radio like nothing before it, with bass, organ, and flutes drawing us into Carl's wispy voice, a theremin and bowed bass chugging alongside the chorus, and counterpoint harmonies passing through like a cleansing rain. It moved like magic from an r&b-based chorus to a stripped-down choral sequence, and was a worldwide number one smash, the only million-selling single the Beach Boys have ever recorded. In Britain's *New Music Express,* the Boys bopped the Beatles in a 1966 popularity poll. Better still, Brian had met Paul—and the digging was mutual! The group went on a British tour, and with the not insignificant help of Derek Taylor, former publicist to the Fabs, were treated like exotic royalty. They hung with the Rolling Stones—image-wise, this was as polar a mixture as night and day—and bought $32,000 cars. Brian had baked his cake and sold it too. "Little Honda," fueled with ambition and amphetamines, was going faster-faster.

Brian's best new friend was David Anderle, and one not insubstantial reason

"So many people think he's the greatest," says his mom. "He is the greatest, and that's very hard to live with." Said his dad: "I taught him everything he knows."

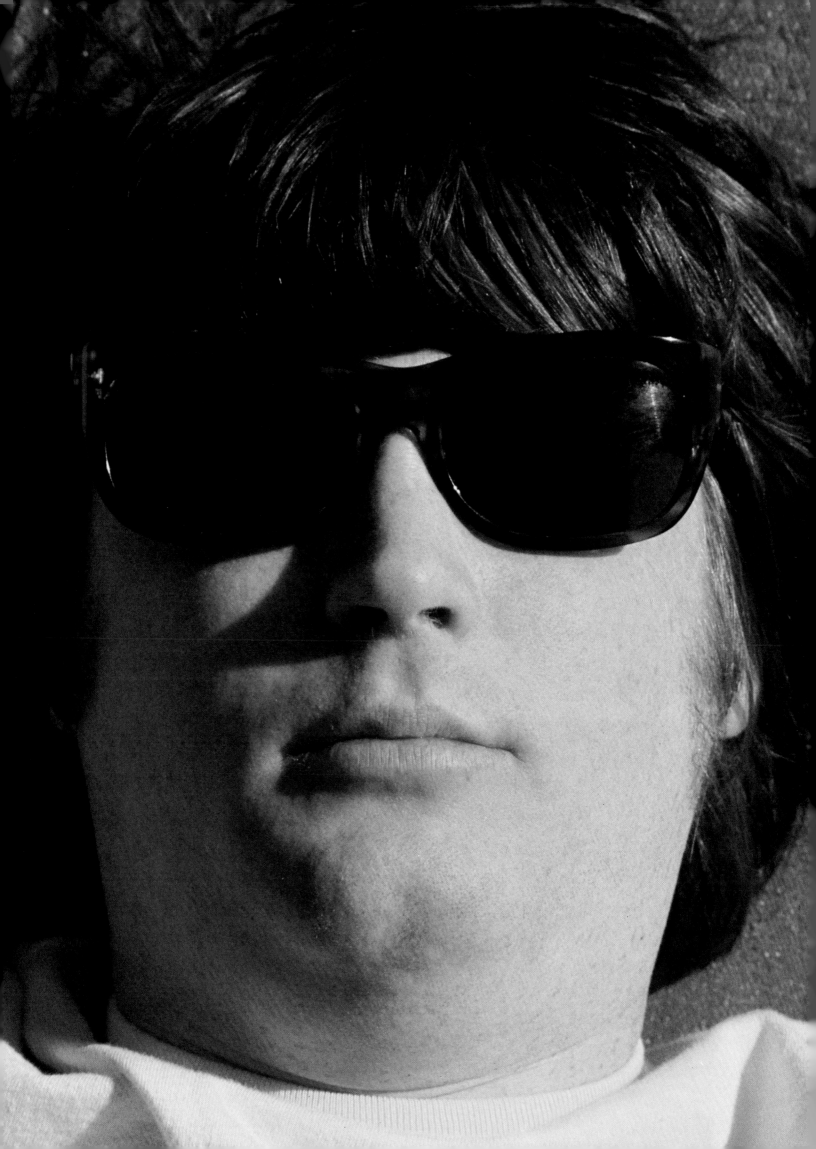

was that in terms of things in and out, Anderle was considered L.A.'s number one hip dude. Anderle was a painter—an art that had mystified Brian—who made his living in and around the music business. One of his management clients was Van Dyke Parks. Brian and Anderle would sit in the pool, as Brian believed that water kept people honest, and conjure counterculture multimedia dreams. They riffed on everything—movies, how you could do radio right, and stores where you could buy telescopes all night long (an idea that occurred one midnight when Brian couldn't satisfy a heavenly craving). They acted on the only one that mattered: music. For true artistic freedom, the Beach Boys, and especially Brian, would need their own record company (the Beatles' Apple was almost two years away). Anderle took on the task of creating Brother Records. Not only would Brother let Brian do anything he wanted, it would also make a lot of money—the first step was to sue Capitol for an audit of back royalties and for a renegotiation of contracts. Relations with the label, which had never been good, would never be the same.

Forget about Oscar and Felix—Brian and Van Dyke, who were now writing songs together, made one odd couple. A Southerner by birth, and an Eastern intellectual by both education and inclination, Parks was about as California as Cambridge. He lived in a Hollywood garage, and one night when Brian asked if he was okay, if he needed anything, Van Dyke said, well, he didn't have a car. At 4 A.M., Brian telephoned Murry, and while the phone lines crackled, told him to send a messenger with a check for $5,000. But the relationship was hardly a one-way street: Van Dyke gave Brian options. Just as he had needed Tony Asher to draft the lyrics to his *Pet Sounds,* Brian required help to step confidently into the even more ambitious work of *Smile.* With Van Dyke on board he could not only compete with the pop bards—the Dylans, the Beatles—but be personally challenged by the most equal collaboration of his career.

Brian liked to entertain friends in his Beverly Hills mansion. At his dining table, a guest would never know quite what to expect. Brian would tap his fork against a glass, and suddenly be directing everybody in a sound poem of cutlery and china. One evening there was a headphone at each place. Shuffling through a stack of thick black acetates, the host invited his guests to preview some tracks from *Smile.* The records were unmarked, but Brian could identify tracks from their distinctive groove patterns, and mumbled "Do You Like Worms" as he slipped the first on the turntable. Rolling timpani introduced a blend of guitar and chants and a seriously silly chant about rocking, rolling and a Plymouth Rock that does the same. Explaining that the track was unfinished, he slipped on an instrumental called "Tones," which lacked a melody line but featured a fetching ensemble of horns bouncing alongside a jaunty clarinet. Horns had never been voiced like this in rock and roll, and wouldn't be until George Martin put town square ornamentation on Beatle songs like "Penny Lane" and "All You Need Is Love." These were separate snatches, explained Brian, that would run together like one big song. He played a track that introduced an

---

Brian produced his wife in a mid-sixties trio called the Honeys, and in an early seventies trio named Spring. None of Brian's outside productions succeeded, largely because he habitually hooked up with artists of such dubious caliber as mid-sixties TV star Paul Peterson. In 1964 he produced the Beach Boys singing his "Pamela Jean" under the name Survivors to see if he could have a hit under a different name. He couldn't. His finest outside production was a 1965 flop single for Glen Campbell, "Guess I'm Dumb," which was on a par with the adventurous work of *Today.*
Murry also tried his hand at independent projects. When the Beach Boys fired him as manager, he put a group called the Sunrays into striped shirts and tried to clone his sons' sound. He couldn't. Murry even conned Capitol into releasing a solo album, *The Many Moods of Murry Wilson.* "Now, it's Murry Wilson's turn!" read part of the liner notes. "You will hear a side of Murry that only his family and close friends are aware of—the songwriter with a flair for melodic structure! And you'll hear a fantastic mixture of sounds uncommon to most recordings!"

Love
Diane Rovell

♡Ginger Blake

To Les,
Love,
Marilyn

RHINO RECORDS

The Honeys

inviting lyrical line with a piano, banjo, and "boing-boing" rhythm: "Light the camp and fire mellow. Cabinessence timely, welcomes the time for a change." A sweet harmonica evoked a friendly tip of a neighbor's hat. That's only part of it, said Brian—he and Van Dyke were building this one so that it would conjure the whole western migration! There would be a section on the building of the railroad ("[Who Ran] The Iron Horse"), and a choral passage depicting another man-made wonder ("[Have You Seen] The Grand Coulee Dam"). The guests were wowed—Brian was onto the big picture here, and he had only to produce the right little pieces for it to fall together.

Stitching things together was nothing new for Brian—*Pet Sounds* had been crafted from separate movements, and "Good Vibrations" had stretched this strategy to dramatic extremes. But *Smile* took one step further: where "Good Vibrations" was a song before it was a production piece, the movements that Brian was composing with Van Dyke were fighting to win themselves a place in an as yet undefined whole. Pieces were written for one context—for instance, a suite of songs dedicated to the barnyard—and subsequently woven into another. But as the acetates piled up, and Brian juggled them this way and that, more of them never found a home. There was an order, Brian believed, that would blend these individual pieces into the cerebral "ooooo" that had been his most soulful sound. But it kept slipping away.

Individual pieces were magnificent. "Our Prayer" was a reverent piece of five-voice *a cappella* that swelled up toward the vaulted ceiling of a prairie cathedral with no roof but the stars. There were no words here, only "aaaas" and "mmmms," but they spoke chapter and verse. Instrumental passages were similarly inspired—a cello sketched a theme called "The Old Master Painter" to

Carl, looking as if he's storing chestnuts in his cheeks, awaiting a vocal cue. As the sweetness drained from Brian's voice, it was left to Carl to sing his brother's leads.

OVERLEAF:

After Carl and Dennis, Bruce Johnston (left) was Brian's biggest fan. He made his first vocal appearance on a Beach Boys' album singing "God Only Knows"—his is the second voice in the round that ends the song.

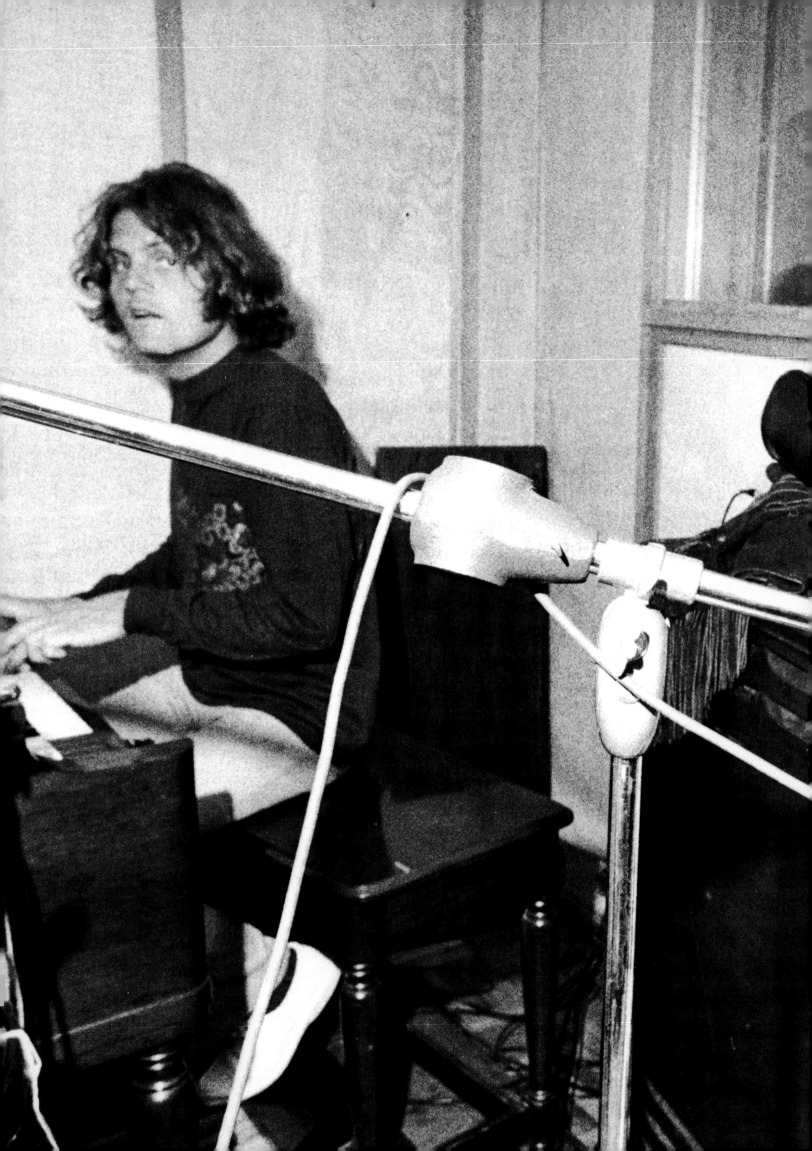

introduce a woozy violin interpreting an earlier summertime standard, "You Are My Sunshine." The cover is appropriate as, still swimming in the backwash of the British Invasion, Brian and Van Dyke were most interested in celebrating America. They also wanted to capture the spirit of nature, and planned an elemental suite that would include a comic book recitation of favored salad stuff ("My Vega-Tables"), a tinkling depiction of the air that we breathe ("Wind Chimes"), and a track that was called "Mrs. O'Leary's Cow" but would forever be known as "Fire."

For "Mrs. O'Leary's Cow" a full string section was called to the studio, where Brian passed out toy firemen's hats and placed a bucket of smoldering wood amidst the players. Atmosphere achieved, he directed the musicians through innumerable takes of a whining crescendo of grinding strings and pounding drums; the music was brutal, foreboding, and evoked the drone of electronic music (not to mention John and Yoko's "Revolution #9," still two years away). Unlike anything else that Brian had ever composed, it spoke with, of all things, bad vibrations. The music thrilled Brian, and scared him too. After it was recorded, he discovered that there had been a rash of fires in the Los Angeles area, which was hardly unusual in a city where brushfires are an annual occurrence. But when a building burned near Western Recorders, Brian, who was prone to fleeting beliefs in everything from astrology to numerology, reportedly attempted but failed to destroy the master tape of "Mrs. O'Leary's Cow." "I don't have to do a big scary fire like that," he said later, as if still fearful of bad magic. "I can do a candle and it's still fire." Candle or fire—they both burn.

"Surf's Up" embodied both the promise and pitfalls of *Smile*. Unlike other songs from that period, it was written during a single session, with Brian discovering the melody at the piano and Van Dyke painting a picture of history that embraces war and peace in the context of innocence denied and redeemed.

On one of a number of bootleg tapes purloined from the *Smile* sessions, Brian can be heard leading a studio ensemble through the song's instrumental track. He's soft-spoken but not spaced-out—just a gifted guy who while not knowing exactly what he wanted would recognize it at once. Take after take, Brian prods the players, refining the tempo and balancing his little rock orchestra across a wide band of the musical spectrum. Most rock crowds the middle with loud drums, bass, and guitar; "Surf's Up" stretched keyboards, bass, and celeste to create a much broader canvas. "That's great," exults Brian, hearing the groove that was once inside his head, and describing the inexplicable as if it were Wendy: "just like jewelry." For the space of a smile, Brian was feeling no pain, but more and more, the walls kept coming closer.

Paul McCartney had been quoted saying that "God Only Knows" was the perfect pop song. Brian, Murry's firstborn son, was frightened—what could he ever do for a follow-up? The Beach Boy who was afraid of the ocean was getting in over his head. The recording studio was in the house now, the final solution to Brian's expensive habit of reserving long blocks of studio time so that he could record on a whim, and lots of people were hanging out. Brian installed a huge red-and-gold tent in the house, like a kid making a fort under a card table, but didn't like the vibes, and rarely stepped inside. He pulled trips on people and took the drugs they offered. Brian fought with Marilyn—she didn't like having her house turned into a studio, and worried about the drugs—while everybody else explained his increasingly paranoid behavior with an indulgent shrug, and an "Oh, that's just Brian."

Brian dreaded recording sessions with the group. Either he'd be frustrated by their renderings of his complex vocal passages and would be forced to sneak back later to sing them himself, or he was assailed with complaints about the material. The lyrics were a particular bone of contention. Mike, for one, objected to lyrics that weren't transparently clear: he recognized that the Beach

Boys had built their reputation with lyrics that a ten-year-old could digest without wrinkling a brow. Mike had sung most of the up-tempo hits; so what was he to make of the lyrics to "Cabinessence?" He asked Parks for clarification on one particular line: "Over and over, the crow cries, uncover the cornfield." "Frankly, Mike," answered Van Dyke, "I don't know what this means. I can't tell you." Mike could dig it when Dylan said (and Al himself had sung on *Party*) that the times were changing, and wanted to be as groovy as the next guy. He just didn't want to blow the bottom line.

Brian wrestled with "Heroes and Villains," juggling pieces of music that sent Van Dyke's Western tale rolling like a tumbleweed alongside the wheels of a stagecoach. One version was said to be twelve minutes long, and to leap beyond the intricacies of "Good Vibrations"; others were much shorter, with jumpy rhythms, or the bottom disappearing under a thick net of floating harmonies. Brian couldn't make up his mind, and there was everything to distract him. He put gym equipment in the living room, and got into watching Johnny Carson. A CBS-TV crew showed up at the house to shoot a sequence about Brian for a network special entitled "Inside Pop: The Rock Revolution." Brian thought that they should film something in the swimming pool, and Murry reportedly jumped into the water. Brian, "a handsome" unshaven "man and baton," was finally cajoled to the piano where he sang "Surf's Up," concluding, "I heard the word, wonderful thing, a children's song." When televised, Brian's performance was framed by Leonard Bernstein's narration, which concluded, "Poetic, beautiful even in its obscurity, 'Surf's Up' is one aspect of new things happening in pop music today." The lyrics, excepting the widely reviled "columnated ruins domino," rang the central Beach Boys theme of childhood innocence in a manner that was worldly and wry. Like Brian's more accessible songs, it would stand the test of time, although timing itself was its very problem. Having made his reputation playing to the top of the pops, Brian was now

Backstage, Mike meditates on the meaning of the
material world.

OVERLEAF:

The one question everybody asks Carl is, "Did you
play the guitar on 'Surfin' U.S.A.'?" His answer is
"yes."

Pickin': Al is the Beach Boys' token folkie—it was he
who steered them toward such songs as "Sloop
John B." and "Cotton Fields."

Brian outside his Bel Air mansion. Originally he
painted it purple, but neighborhood pressure
pushed him back to a neutral shade.

FACING PAGE:

''Carl and I were into prayer,'' says Brian of their
closeness during the recording of *Pet Sounds.* ''We
prayed for light and guidance through the album.
We kind of made it a religious ceremony.''

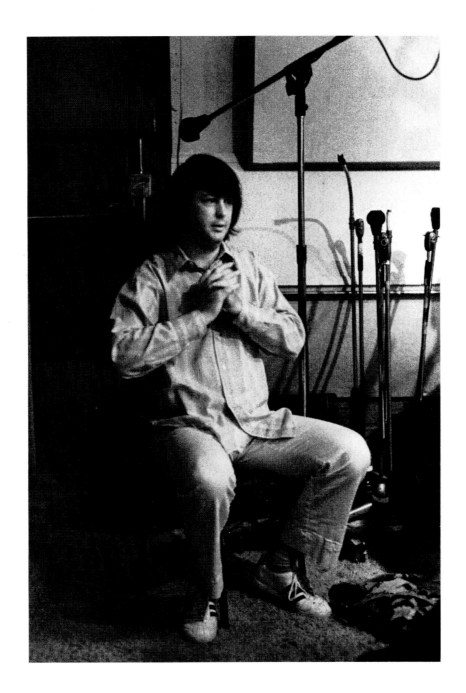

OVERLEAF:

Insiders offer different reports on Brian's songwriting activity during the seventies. He's said to have written dozens of songs that have never been released. Some say that he is afraid, if not unable, to pursue a song to its ultimate conclusion. One thing's for sure: if he'd written a commercial-sounding hit, we'd have heard it.

writing to a cult group—the burgeoning counterculture. Kids didn't yet take themselves quite so seriously (the Summer of Love was still a season away), and as far as the group and their mass audience was concerned, fun was in, and art was for museums.

As 1966 turned into 1967, the advance word on *Smile* was that it would change the face of rock and roll. Capitol produced an album cover (catalog number 2580), and at Brian's insistence prepared an illustrated folio to be included in the package. Ads were placed in the music trades. The only problem was that *Smile* was still in pieces. "Good Vibrations" had once been in many pieces, but Brian had eventually felt it hit the pocket. *Smile,* as elusive as the one on the print of Mona Lisa that hung in Brian's living room, confounded the man who had given new meaning to fun.

Beautiful even in its obscurity. In their own convoluted way, those words say as much about the Beach Boys as fun, fun, fun. "I've been in this town so long that back in the city I've been taken for lost and gone and I've known for a long, long time." Versions of "Heroes and Villains" were beginning to clutter the studio. Brian kept trying just one more. Anderle, hip-deep in business plans, was forced to come on like Capitol: Brian, he said, Brothers Records needs a single. Brian felt betrayed—all he had ever heard about was product. Anderle was left outside Brian's room, fruitlessly begging for his friend to open the door. Parks, who had stifled his own formidable ego to collaborate with Brian, was offended by his partner's less than steadfast support of the lyrics. When Warner Brothers offered him a contract for a solo album, Van Dyke was lost and gone. "Once at night, Catillion Square was light, she was right in the rain of bullets that eventually would bring her down." Hollywood had come and gone from Hawthorne, and Brian was alone and, as always, in familiar surroundings: his brothers, Murry, Mike, Capitol, and the extended Beach Boys family. "Sure, Brian," they said, "this music is far out, but . . ." Without the necessary support system, Brian did what he always did—retreated. One night he went to a movie called *Seconds* and was rattled that the first words from the screen were "Hello, Mr. Wilson." It was the brain police, led by an antagonized Phil Spector, trying to invade his mind. People were spying on him and his project called *Smile*—maybe even the Beatles! "But she's still dancing in the night unafraid of what a dude would do in a town full of heroes and villains." Brian danced into his room and closed the door.

Smile was never released; it was never even completed. Instead of being Brian's intended masterpiece, it became the most famous unreleased album in the history of rock. The LP called the Beach Boys on all the bets they had placed on art, blood, and money. And they crapped out. "When the promise is broken," wrote Bruce Springsteen, who named the girl Wendy in his own "Born to Run," "you go on living, but man it takes something from down in your soul." Writing a decade later, and from a beach town clear across the continent, Springsteen's unreleased song "The Promise" could just as well be the story of the Beach Boys. By backing down from the challenge of *Smile,* the group denied themselves a future beyond their past. They would never again sing so sweetly. Brian, along with everybody else who loved the Beach Boys, would have to live with Springsteen's final denouement: "Like when the truth is spoken, and it don't make no difference, something in your heart grows cold."

From wave one, the Beach Boys have acted like most show biz families and kept their wagons in a circle. Outsiders were suspect until they were proven innocent. "Even to this day," said Murry in 1971, "when a son comes off and starts giving me a Hollywood approach, I say, 'What are you doing, coming off phony, Hollywood, baby?' Right down their throat. I keep at them, beating their eardrums, because I know that fame and fortune might distort them."

OVERLEAF:

Dennis, the outsider as a kid, would remain the loner as a man. He was always the first to declare his independence from the group. Here he's pictured during the shooting of *Two-Lane Blacktop,* a 1971 cult film in which he starred with the equally deadpan James Taylor.

When Brian left the road, the unity of the circle was disturbed. Brian would always be a brother, but home alone, he would also be the center of his own circle. To the Beach Boys, *Smile* sounded like a Brian Wilson solo album: more than ever, they were cast as the composer's instruments. But group members didn't make solo albums in 1966, and even more, the Beach Boys were not a group without Brian. As much as Brian has always needed his family, they've always needed him more.

The Beach Boys now lived grown-up, complicated lives. Dennis was leaving his first wife and having to work harder to render his life in triplicate fun. Mike, already into his second marriage, was aware that a pop star's salary had to keep pace with both alimony and a by-now routinely extravagant lifestyle. As green rookies, members of the group were happy to glide upon Brian's guidance. *Pet Sounds* had created friction—Mike had referred to it as "Brian's ego music," and its commercial failure had solidified his desire to not "fuck with the formula." The even bigger commercial gamble of *Smile* intensified the group's doubts: maybe Brian didn't always know best? For five years the art of the Beach Boys had meshed seamlessly with the demands of the marketplace. Sensing that their captain was now leading them astray, the crew mutinied and cut their boat adrift.

The release of *Smile* in early 1967 would have dramatically changed the story of the Beach Boys. It would have immediately solved their problem with hip: whatever its commercial fate, the album would have revealed a band at the forefront of the burgeoning counterculture. Instead, lacking the support of both his old group and his newly departed Hollywood friends, a frustrated Brian drifted deeper into acid and speed, and the LP was left to languish. In June of 1967, the Beatles greeted the Summer of Love with *Sgt. Pepper's Lonely Hearts Club Band,* an album that received the type of high-art accolades that Brian had envisioned for himself. Painfully aware that he could have beaten the Beatles to the punch, Brian's *Smile* turned into a frown, and things turned from bad to worse. At the last minute the Beach Boys dropped out of the Monterey Pop Festival, a forum where they might have proven that the original California band could compete with the burgeoning "San Francisco sound." By the time the hippies got a headful of Janis Joplin and the Jefferson Airplane, the Beach Boys were history. Or as festival breakout Jimi Hendrix put it, "you'll never hear surf music again."

The standard line is·that Brian went one toke over the line during the production of *Smile* and emerged a hermetic acid casualty. Reports of his behavior did little to dispel this notion, and in the intervening years the official Beach Boys line has laid the blame squarely on acid and amphetamines. Drugs undoubtedly helped to unhinge Brian, whose personality had always been tethered between awkward and isolated, but this explanation is much too pat, and more in keeping with a parental view of the world than that of a brother (figurative or literal). The likely truth is even whorier—drugs offered Brian escape from a battle that pitted his artist's soul against his family obligations. As an artist, he wanted to grow; as his family's provider, he was encouraged to stay the same. The choice was clear: be an artist or be a good son. Abandon responsibility—that is, leave home—or do your job for the family. Brian went back to his room and settled for neither.

Instead of releasing the album called *Smile,* the Beach Boys dribbled out the material over the next five years, and they were invariably the aesthetic highlights of their respective LPs. First came *Smiley Smile,* which included simplified versions of "Wind Chimes," "Wonderful," "Vega-Tables," and the single releases of "Good Vibrations" and "Heroes and Villains." Two years later, in 1969, "Cabinessence" and "Our Prayer" were included on *20/20,* the group's last album for Capitol. The next year, part of the elemental suite, the water section entitled "I Love to Say Da-Da," was incorporated into "Cool Water."

OVERLEAF:

The Beach Boys gained some much-needed counterculture credibility with their appearance at the Big Sur Folk Festival in 1970, where they were joined onstage by Mimi Fariña.

And finally, on the 1972 album that bore its name, the world got to hear (over Brian's objections) what was probably the greatest song to emerge from the Wilson-Parks partnership: "Surf's Up." Spliced together, these tracks make for a whale of an album, and their piecemeal release damnably emphasized the group's fatal failure of nerve. The rationing of Brian's work from the turn of 1967 created the illusion that Brian was a fully functioning member of the group. In fact, his participation in the studio was on a steady decline—*Smile* had already broken his heart, and once was enough. There is no reason to believe that the "Cabinessence" on *20/20* is at all like what Brian would have released. Everything depended on the way one shuffled the cards. What we have is bold and beautiful; what we lost we'll never know.

The Beach Boys had effectively squandered the critical momentum that they had won with *Pet Sounds* and capitalized on with "Good Vibrations." "Heroes and Villains" was released a full eight months after "Good Vibrations," and, in terms of both art and commerce, fell into its shadow. A dense and engaging piece of work, there was the distinct sense that it had fallen shy of the pocket. Brian, the bass player, had let it go without a solid foundation, and heaven knows what else. For the first time in his career, Brian had settled on a song that was less than his best. It wouldn't be the last.

Without the unencumbered leadership of Brian, the Beach Boys became a democracy without vision, a competent band instead of an inspired one. Rock bands are rarely true democracies—John and Paul ruled the Beatles much as Mick Jagger and Keith Richards commanded the Rolling Stones—but the Beach Boys weren't even a partnership. They were a monarchy. In the end, the ebb and flow of their career is a testament to the wide gap of talent between Brian and his mates. A similar situation ruined another great band of the late sixties: Creedence Clearwater Revival. After Creedence had scored a string of hits with trenchant songs by singer-guitarist John Fogerty, other members of

FOLLOWING SPREADS:

Dennis and crew at Brother Records studio in Santa Monica, 1976. The studio has since been sold. Dennis's 1977 solo album, *Pacific Ocean Blue,* gathered good reviews and sold a respectable 200,000 copies. Carl followed with two albums of his own. Brian has released one solo 45: "Caroline, No."

Dennis smooches, Audree looks away, and Annie Leibovitz searches for a picture.

Carl and Annie Wilson, 1975, in a rented beach house. Since the mid-seventies Carl's primary residence has been in Colorado.

Mike enjoys an audience with Maharishi Mahesh Yogi. During a 1976 interview with Mike Douglas, Brian broke the rules by revealing his personal mantra to the television audience.

I'm Dennis Wilson and you're not. Chevy Chase, who knows from cameras, cops a free Heineken backstage in Anaheim.

the quartet won the righteous right to sing and write for Creedence albums. As with the Beach Boys, democracy among unequal artists diminished the whole. Creedence broke up after one more disastrous album, the victims of their own success. Fogerty withdrew from the spotlight and remains, like Brian, one of rock's great lost living artists. But the two men are not at all similar: Creedence became history, and Fogerty went off to live an independent life in the Northwest. The Beach Boys lived on, even if Brian had dropped out of active service and acted pretty weird to boot. One thing about Brian—he'd never leave home. One other thing—he'd always be a Beach Boy.

From 1967 until 1972, as if on sheer momentum, the Beach Boys produced solid albums that sank like stones. *Smiley Smile,* whose very title bastardized the LP Brian couldn't bring himself to complete, set the precedent: it was the first album produced by the entire group. Brian was tired of doing everything, and couldn't be counted on anyway; Carl, who had been learning from Brian since he was knee-high, took on a more central role. Recorded at Brian's home studio in a month, the LP substituted minimalism for the rich complexities of its namesake, and sounded feeble given the expectations generated by "Good Vibrations" (included by the authority of Capitol, à la "Sloop John B.") and the general hype on *Smile.* Carl has the last word: "It was a bunt instead of a grand slam." (Soon thereafter, Van Dyke Parks released *Song Cycle,* a critical success and commercial bomb that suggested *Smile* in both its construction and American theme.) *Wild Honey,* released just two months later, was a home-baked band record of r&b-based songs with everybody playing his own instrument. "Darling" was wonderful, the title tune sweet soul music, and the rest was good-natured fun. The only problem was, Brian neglected his best genre of soul—avant-garde r&b.

With record sales plummeting, Capitol cranked out volumes II and III of the greatest hits series, and a boxed set of three albums from '65 and '66. Increas-

Being a very spiritual guy, when Mike married Cathy
he took her to the very font of rock 'n' religiosity—
Wolfman Jack.

ingly dependent on concert revenue, their shows similarly relied on oldies—the new stuff rarely roused the concert crowds. What's worse, their U.S. audience was on the decline. Back in Bel Air, Brian was troubled and would disappear into his room for long periods of time. Marilyn couldn't draw him out of it, and neither could his family, who ignored it as best they could. Brian would soon become the father of two daughters, Carnie and Wendy, the first born in 1968. Brian told Marilyn one thing upfront: she would have to be the disciplinarian. He didn't trust himself. Brian was no longer the father in the larger Beach Boys constellation; he was back to being Murry's failed son. To the public, he became the reclusive genius. One minute he was running a Hollywood health food store called the Radiant Radish, the next he was crazy Brian in a bathrobe, hidden in the shadows in the back of a limousine. Two limos pull up to a stop at the same Beverly Hills traffic light. The smoked passenger window of one whirls downward, and the voice of Phil Spector is heard: "Hello, Mr. Wilson."

The pressure was on the Beach Boys, who were now weathering the tough times that they had skipped when they were young. In December of '67, the group returned to London after a UNICEF benefit in Paris. The phone rang—it was Dennis, who had lingered in France, saying that they had to come back and meet this guy Maharishi Mahesh Yogi, and dig on his Transcendental Meditation. Mike, Carl, and Al returned and made meditation into a lifelong habit. Not Dennis. Mike got really transported, traveling to India alongside the Beatles and thinking of ways by which the Beach Boys could encourage meditation. "I didn't want to live life at the same level twenty years from now," says Mike of his initial attraction to TM. "And one of the greatest things that interested me is that he (Maharishi) said, 'You don't have to give up your Rolls-Royce . . . and forsake all the pursuits of material pleasures . . . to develop inner spiritual qualities.' That sounded real good to me." Soon thereafter the Beatles

Says Beach Boys fan Eric Carmen, ''Their vocal harmonies are unsurpassed . . . I think Brian was a French horn, Carl was a flute, Al Jardine a trumpet, Dennis a trombone, and Mike Love a baritone sax before their present incarnation as the Beach Boys.''

OVERLEAF:

Dennis and Christine McVie of Fleetwood Mac had a tumultuous romance from 1979 to 1981. ''Half of him was a little boy,'' says McVie, ''and the other half was insane.'' Either he'd storm through her house in a drunken rage or hire a symphony orchestra to help him serenade her with ''You Are So Beautiful.''

would abandon the Indian spiritualist, and John Lennon would make him a laughingstock in "Sexy Sadie." The Beach Boys remained loyal, and lost a small fortune and substantial fan support by mounting a shared-bill tour with the Maharishi that lasted about the length of your average mantra.

The following spring, back in Los Angeles, Dennis picked up a couple of women hitchhiking, stashed them at his mansion on Sunset Boulevard, and continued on to a recording session. He returned to find himself with a dozen houseguests. Charles Manson, the brainwashing acid guru of a small band of mostly female loyalists, held out his hand. Dennis, the sexy Beach Boy, was not a man to ignore his libido, and thought it just deserts for a new bachelor to be serviced by a harem of hippies. The freeloading didn't bother him either—Dennis was generous to a fault, a quality some friends attributed to a feeling of guilt about his pop star wealth. Plus there was no resisting Charlie, an aspiring songwriter who could talk rings around Saturn and seemed to be able to push anybody's buttons. "Sometimes," Dennis told England's *Rave* magazine, speaking of Manson, "the wizard frightens me." For Dennis, fascination has always been the flip side of fright. Dennis was encouraged to take Charlie's songs to the Beach Boys under his own name. Manson trusted Dennis for the money—hell, the "Family" had probably already squeezed him for $100,000, and that's not counting the uninsured Mercedes they'd totaled. Dennis changed the name of one of the songs to "Never Learn Not To Love," and the draggy dirge appeared on the Beach Boys' *20/20,* their last contracted album for Capitol. On Manson's own album, the song is called "Cease to Exist."

By the fall, the Family scene was getting a little freaky for Dennis, so he moved into a basement room of a friend's house and, characteristically, called the business people to clean up his mess. Booted out of the mansion, Charlie was not pleased, and when encountering Dennis would spit out increasingly venomous raps: the end was near, blacks were going to take over, and Manson

As Dennis grew older, his hard living began to show and the fair-haired boy became a rough-hewn man. Here he is photographed by old friend Dean Torrence.

Just as the Wilson family would be central to the
history of the Beach Boys, so would each of the
group seek solace in his own family. Dennis is
pictured with Karen Lamm, his stormiest relationship
in a life that saw little romantic stability. After a
1976 New Year's Eve concert, Mike visits with his
children from various marriages. Brian, who during
his worst periods was more of a child than a father,
takes his two daughters and two of Carl's kids for a
backstage spin in Anaheim.

OVERLEAF:

Far from Hawthorne, Brian and Marilyn look on as
Carnie gets a Beverly Hills make-over.

would come back to rule. Then Charlie would ask Dennis for money. Dennis avoided him altogether until the fall of 1969, when Manson was revealed to have led the ceremonial slaughter thereafter codified as the Tate-LaBianca murders. The night of his arrest, Manson vainly tried to contact Dennis for help. Death threats against the drummer and his son were relayed to dissuade Dennis from testifying at the Family's trial (it worked, although others corroborated whatever he knew). Dennis became increasingly jumpy, and no wonder—members of the Family would reportedly sneak into his house at night and rearrange the furniture.

Dennis had met Charlie in a place where a dream could be twisted into a nightmare. Smog had settled over Los Angeles, and after Manson, America added another image to its Southern California consciousness—random violence. In the East, you'd get shot by somebody in your family. In the new California a loved one might plug you, but you might also be chopped up by a stranger, stuffed into a plastic bag, and left by the side of the interchange. L.A. had a new favorite band, the Doors, and singer Jim Morrison was more about midnight than meditation. In a long set piece called "The End," Morrison was an Oedipal Manson confronting his dad: "Father?" "Yes, son." "I want to kill you." Crosby, Stills, Nash and Young was the big new harmony group, with strong past affiliations (the Byrds, Buffalo Springfield, and the Hollies), innocuous music, and a natural bond to the counterculture. Nobody could ever again capture California with the authority of the early Beach Boys; the Golden State had become much too complicated.

In 1968, a year in U.S. history that read like choreographed trauma, the Beach Boys released *Friends,* an album so laid back some thought it asleep. "We've been good friends now for so many years." The title song made welcome with voices that were like fraternal slaps on the back. The Beach Boys devotee is innocent by nature, and is glad to grab at straws while imagining

"Good Timin'," from 1979's *M.I.U. Album,* is the
prettiest song the Beach Boys have recorded in a
decade.

FACING PAGE:

As Dennis's drinking and drug habits worsened, he
became an erratic concert performer. With another
drummer keeping time, he'd sometimes seem lost on
a big stage.

ABOVE:

While old fans relished the opportunity to see Brian
back onstage, it could also be a painful experience.
His voice was racked by cigarettes and other bad
habits. Because he'd sometimes play a different
song, he was often given an inaudible piano.

OVERLEAF:

In 1981 Carl threatened to leave the group unless
they rehearsed more and worked on new music. He
told *Rolling Stone,* "The Beach Boys' show puts itself
on. All we have to do is show up. We can do a real
turkey of a set and people will come back and say,
'That's the greatest show I've ever seen.' "

the band's return to full glory. *Friends* is a wholly likable record that has aged remarkably well; the seed of its amiability, however, is that it had nothing to do with ambition. Life is good, and music is a comfort. Brian no longer sought to dazzle, and by themselves the group could be no more than amiable. Cynics and the ever-faithful agreed: Brian's "Busy Doin' Nothin'" was the sad but true heart of *Friends*. Over a bossa nova beat buttered by clarinets, Brian tells us about a day in the life: "I get a lotta thoughts in the morning, I write 'em all down; If it wasn't for that, I'd forget 'em in a while." On the phone Brian invites us all over to visit, and practically draws a map. "You'll turn left on a little road, it's a bumpy one." Upon arrival, we'd find Brian "keeping busy while I wait." But nobody ever comes. The song ends with Brian dialing a number—nobody's home—and sitting down to write a letter to the absent friend. Was this West Coast existentialism—L'Etranger de L.A.—or just plain dumb?

"Do It Again" was released in the summer of '68, and the message was by now obvious: nostalgia would be the fulcrum of the Beach Boys' future. They'd toast the summer again, and again. A chunky bass beat opens the song, hot-wiring the rhythm as if it were '64, but disappears long before the end. Brian was a great believer in the importance of tags—that the end of a song should be a musical high—but here forgot one of the loudest bass hooks of his career. Sabotage? Brian knew that if it were perfect—that is, if it were a hit—they'd just want another. Not that Brian didn't want the Beach Boys to have hits—he even went so far as to write a summer single called "Breakaway" with Murry

FACING PAGE:

Dennis's 1977 solo album, *Pacific Ocean Blue*, gathered good reviews and sold a respectable 200,000. Carl followed with two albums of his own. Brian has released one solo 45: "Caroline No."

OVERLEAF:

Once the Beach Boys bit the bullet and succumbed to their past, the fans lost any expectations concerning their future. It was enough to simply celebrate the spirit of summertime.

In late 1966, Capitol Records printed two covers for
Smile, prepared an illustrated promotional booklet
to be included, and began a program of prerelease
promotion. It remains the most famous unreleased LP
in the history of rock.

(aka, "Reggie Dunbar"). But Brian was older now, and it was easier to act like an adolescent than to make it ring true. Brian had never been a surfer, but he could imagine himself hanging ten. Grown up, and weary from the effort, he found that the language of fun had become strangely foreign.

Amidst the rock boom of the sixties, many a successful rock band blew the pot on bad business and high living. As pop pioneers, the Beach Boys set appropriate precedents. Murry drove Capitol crazy, practically setting up camp at the Tower offices, but fought more from heart than experience. He was followed by a long chain of managerial associations that, like the group itself, acted as if the hits would never stop. In the late sixties the Beach Boys tottered on bankruptcy. They were far from needy, to be sure, but considering the sixty-odd-million records that they'd already sold, they were less than rock-solid. Royalty litigation with Capitol went on for years. Brother Records lasted one release on the label *(Smiley Smile)* and disappeared until 1970, when it was reactivated upon the Beach Boys' move to Warner Brothers. No bit of business, however, packed the symbolic punch of Murry's sale of Sea of Tunes Music, publisher of the golden-era songs of the Beach Boys, to A&M Records. Murry's income derived from the publishing royalties of Brian's songs, which is why he complained bitterly about the tenor of his son's post-"California Girls" music. Murry sold, at presumably less than top dollar, when the catalog was at low tide. No matter what he got, A&M got more: revenue from millions of repackaged hits albums that Capitol sold in the seventies, and steady money from Madison Avenue's annual revival of ads that make those hits into summertime jingles. Business aside, the deal also smacked of blood: Murry didn't tell Brian or the Beach Boys that he was selling the catalog. Maybe he knew that they couldn't afford to buy, or maybe he didn't want to look into his son's eyes once he had decided that the game was now over and it was time to cash in the chips.

SUNFLOWER, THE BEACH BOYS' 1970 WARNER BROTHERS DEBUT, offered the group a golden opportunity for revitalization. Warners gave the band something they'd lacked since at least 1965—a support system willing to sell them as valid contemporary artists. At Capitol they were the good-time kids from Hawthorne, and through a decade that saw the pop world practically reinvented, the company did little to change their marketing strategy. For their own part, the Beach Boys even considered changing their name. Warners recognized that the success of the Beach Boys was contingent on Brian's participation, and could only have been encouraged by what they heard. Though production was credited to the group, *Sunflower* glowed with the care and intensity of a Brian Wilson production, and according to Bruce Johnston was the last Beach Boys album in which everybody participated and Brian called the shots. Johnston once lamented that people considered the Beach Boys "surfing Doris Days," and indeed the Technicolor sound of *Sunflower* reflected the privileged life of the Hollywood bourgeoisie. This was an adult rock and roll album made by men who had been Beach Boys for nine years.

"Add Some Music to Your Day," a single released in front of the LP, reintroduced the voices of America's youth within a lyric corny enough for Disneyland. The lead vocal was passed among the group (in order: Mike, Bruce, Brian, Dennis, Carl, Al), offering touching points in contrast, particularly between Brian, whose voice had gone raspy at the edges, and Carl, who had absorbed a measure of his brother's sweetness. (Individual portraits on the cover offered similar comparisons, with a white-robed Mike receiving children like a guru, and Brian grinning from under a hat that says "Good Humor.") The song recites the places where one encounters music, and implies that this is one art form that can't be defined by words or intellectual notions: "music is in my

The boys who are forevermore men.

soul." The goal of *Sunflower* would be to brighten the day. No pretensions—just pretty.

Brian's all over *Sunflower,* writing half of it with various Beach Boys and following through with an attention to sound and arrangement that had been dormant since *Pet Sounds.* Recorded in ambient stereo, everybody shines under a thick lattice of vocal arrangements, especially Dennis, who opens the album with the best song of his career, "Slip On Through." A moo-cow plea from a guy to his girl, the track enters the realm of the spiritual "oooo" on the rolling momentum of voices that glimmer and glow. Almost as good is his side-closing "It's About Time," which transcends verbal mumbo jumbo with a jam featuring Carl's heaviest guitar since "Surfin' U.S.A." Breaking with Beach Boys tradition, *Sunflower* was a stylish celebration of adult fun. Johnston's songs are straight from the mushy heart of Hollywood, and within this plush context are as shiny as the Rolls he's pictured with, especially "Deirdre," draped by Brian in a luxurious veil of harmony. Brian's other songs burn with low-key assurance, ranging from the mellow court and spark of "All I Wanna Do" to the more ambitious tone poem of "Cool, Cool, Water," a playful hymn to the Beach Boys' favorite cluster of atoms, which drew a chanted backdrop from the composer's long-abandoned elemental suite.

In one minute, fifty-five seconds, Brian's one solo composition, "This Whole World," swept years of bad memories off the floor. For the first time since he was running full tilt with Van Dyke, Brian was at one with the wind, and in a rush of joy the copious stories of his acid-casualty state sprayed the air like jetsam. Make no mistake, Brian was not out of the woods, but for one shining moment he let us know that an artist can lose his way but retain his spirit. Based on a typically Brian homily that equates romantic love to world peace, it finds Carl's lead voice flying atop an undulating carpet of shifting voices and textures that coalesce into a twenty-second tag that chills the spine: a falsetto glissando is buttressed by the "aum-bop-ditdit" underpinning that runs throughout the song, and is then joined by a third harmonic counterpoint restating the title. There was nothing elusive about the beauty of "This Whole World"; it was bold and bright as the sun. Once again, Brian had created a song filled with wonder.

Sunflower was another home run that died in the stores, and the specter of *Smile* reared its head: how could America's biggest-selling rock group be satisfied with making artful music for anything but the masses? The difference, however, is telling: in 1966 the lack of numbers reflected the larval stages of a pop audience attuned to more than the Top 40, but by 1970 dozens of artists had found success in the less commercial format. *Sunflower* simply failed to find a niche: in an age of denim, it sounded like alligator shirts. Woodstock had happened, Nixon was in the White House, and the counterculture had spilled out into the streets. *Sunflower* was an album of privilege painted in pastels, and was certainly not the record to slap on the stereo while waiting for the mescaline to hit. Brian was past the point of caring—his spirit had long been dashed, and he felt himself a fool for having been suckered back into this Beach Boys game. Cocaine was so much easier; in lonely retreat, Brian went back to sleep.

The Beach Boys, their critical reputation bolstered and live shows invigorated by *Sunflower,* were again up the creek without a paddle. Jack Rieley, a Pacifica deejay who boasted of everything from a Pulitzer Prize to writing regularly for *Psychology Today,* talked quick solutions to the Beach Boys' image problems and became their publicist, and then their manager. Rieley's strategy was for the Beach Boys to make peace with the counterculture by becoming relevant. (Carl was similarly making peace with the government—in 1967 he'd been indicted for refusing induction into the army. Five years in court were required for acceptance of both his status as religious conscientious objector and

---

OVERLEAF:

If Brian, who dislikes the ocean, had written a song called "Till I Dive," the first line might've been, "I'm a cork in a swimming pool."

proposed alternative service: free Beach Boys concerts at hospitals, orphanages, and prisons.) It was no longer enough to sing of the warmth of the sun; the Beach Boys would instead preach about the ecology. They would play benefits for the people, and perform in Washington before a May Day crowd, placing plastic words of protest onto the Coasters' "Riot in Cell Block Number 9" and calling it "Student Demonstration Time." This was not Brian converting a Chuck Berry tune into a super-stock surf anthem, but a calculated gambit that rang hollow and dull. The album would be called *Landlocked,* but without Brian in the center ring the cohesiveness of the *Sunflower* sessions was gone. As Dennis had pushed the ball over the goal line with his songs for the last album, Carl, working alone in the studio like brother Brian of old, constructed two cornerstones ("Feel Flows" and "Long Promised Road") for the new LP. The fact of the matter, though, was that Carl's best work merely alluded to what Brian had once delivered. Again, as always, the Beach Boys needed their big brother, and as he was out to lunch, they went back once more to pick the carcass of *Smile.* (Actually, *Smile* had been a tangential element in the band's move to Warners, with Carl pledging to piece it together for eventual release; that he never followed through leaves the impression that the album remains more valuable to the Beach Boys as a continuing myth than as a realized piece of pop art.)

PRECEDING SPREAD:

Through the years, the Beach Boys have fought like dogs but stuck together like family.

Brian's childhood friend Rich Sloan recalls that "Brian's dad always used to be really interested in Brian's athletic ability; he used to stand on the left-field sideline and tell Brian where to play."

OVERLEAF:

Included in the schedule Dr. Landy imposes on Brian is mandatory time at the piano. Once upon a time, Brian could not be torn away from his music. He's younger than that now.

"Surf's Up," which would quickly become the new album's title song, featured the Beach Boys singing along with the vocal Brian had recorded years earlier for the CBS documentary, and tagging it with another Wilson-Parks snippet, "Child Is The Father To Man." The desired impression was that Brian had climbed back on the horse and was willing to exert his artistry. The truth was that the thoroughbred had bolted, and the jockey had packed away his silks. Brian reportedly broke down crying when Dennis told him of the rescue of his legendary gem, and begged him to stop its release. "We need that song for the new album," countered his brother. "We need it—goddammit, don't you understand?" Brian understood all too well, and watched while he was made to look as if he were at the center of a group he no longer thought of as his own. He cut long lines of cocaine, and strung them together as if they were melodies.

"I'm a cork on the ocean," sang Brian, characteristically putting his heart into his one solo song, "Till I Die," and it cried real tears on an album that was emotionally mute. The song evoked extreme helplessness as a hungry heart ebbed and flowed until it was dashed against a rocky shore. "How deep is the ocean? I lost my way." Rieley had steered the boat into the seventies, but by hooking his strategy onto a transitory notion of what's hip today had effectively denied the group its aura of timelessness. The Beach Boys were only as relevant as their vision was clear, and if Brian couldn't get out of bed but to write a silly jingle called "Jack Rieley is not Superman," they swung with a substitute savior who could at least promise them the moon, if not deliver—Rieley's business moves were as bad as the validity of his credentials, and Carl fired him a year later.

Paul McCartney was in town, his old group kaput and Wings quickly off the ground, and he wanted to hang out with his second-favorite bass player. Brian cowered at the thought—What had he written to supplant "God Only

Dennis and Gage, his son by Shawn Love. Dennis
was also the father of two sons and a daughter from
previous marriages.

Knows"? Nothing!—and hid in a poolside cabana at the house in Bel Air. Paul tapped on the door, lightly, and attempted to console the frightened Beach Boy with his soft Beatles brogue. The door remained closed, and as Paul stood sentry, Brian wept.

Murry Wilson died of a heart attack on June 4, 1973. The sons reacted as their father had taught: Brian hopped on a plane to New York, Dennis sank into a depression broken by violent shifts of mood, and Carl added another wrinkle to his Buddha brow. Since *Surf's Up,* the Beach Boys had produced two abysmal albums, *So Tough* (which Warners copackaged with *Pet Sounds,* as if in apology) and *Holland,* with barely a spark contributed by Brian. *Holland* was initially rejected by Warners, who asked Van Dyke Parks, then a company VP, to see whether he could shake a single out of his old friend. Years later, Parks would say, "I'd like to catch Brian out in the yard so I could get into a little kick-ass with him. I think he's misbehaved. It's as simple as that. He's just very talented, and I think he's perpetuated a great myth." On this day, Parks kicked ass. "Write a middle eight," he instructed Brian, who replied with a question: "Do you think I'm crazy?" "Brian," said Van Dyke, "write a middle eight!" What emerged was "Sail On Sailor," by far the best song on *Holland.*

Parks might have been able to pull a melody out of his troubled friend, but like the others who would try, he couldn't coax Brian to stand up for himself. Brian had always put out for other people—as a kid he was quick to go along with the guys, and later he made everybody millions writing hits for the Beach Boys. Finally, when everybody told him he was being selfish, he stopped writing his own music. He'd habitually dabble at the piano, but his songs had become sketches, and got no farther. Why bother? It certainly wouldn't matter to Brian, fat and dirty, a scared and mangy bear in a thick terrycloth robe. Brian walks into the Troubadour wearing red pajamas, a bathrobe, and floppy bedroom slippers. He pounds his thighs to the fusion beat being put out by jazz guitarist Larry Coryell's group, and in a fit of excitement tumbles onto the stage to howl . . . "Be-Bop-A-Lula." Brian is hustled out a side exit. It's midnight in L.A., and somewhere up in the hills, locked into his own mansion, Phil Spector plays with a pistol and hums an old tune. Prisoners of their own past, the two men haunt a town built for right now, and condemn themselves to an aborted present, where growth is out of the question and regression is nothing to die over. An "eccentric burnout," at least he knew where he stood, not like when Murry burst into the room after Brian had written "Surfin' U.S.A." and shouted that the tempo was terrible. Brian told his father to go to hell. Now he felt bad. "He cried when he heard my voice," recalled Murry's first son. "But I can't walk backwards, go back to him, and sing a song for him." Brian no longer needed Murry—he knew how to hurt himself.

The Beach Boys had long battled over their live show, with Carl insisting that a constant updating was necessary, and Mike fighting to give the people what they seemed to want: an in-concert jukebox. In June of '74 Capitol released *Endless Summer,* a two-record set of early hits, and the conflict became academic. Like the *Spirit of America* set that followed the next year, Brian's collected hits sold in the millions. Lacking new product, Warner countered with a post-'65 hits album, and double-set repackages of the late-sixties LPs that the group had wrested from Capitol during litigation. But these caused comparatively minor ripples; Capitol still owned the candy store. Peter Pans in a grown-up world, the Beach Boys were forced to admit that their only future was in their past, and became a major concert draw because their nostalgia rang so true and was desired so desperately. They became *Rolling Stone*'s band of the year in 1974, the year of Watergate, and on a major tour with Chicago blew

OVERLEAF:

Dr. Eugene Landy became Brian's new dad, the disciplinarian determined to straighten out his life and make him, once again, the raison d'être of the Beach Boys. Like Murry, Landy has never acted as if Brian might be better off outside the group.

Brian forever dances alongside the stuff of his past: the sounds of the surf, and the songs that will not die.

away the competition like Mrs. O'Leary's cow. (Chicago manager-producer Jim Guercio briefly became the Beach Boys' manager and did double-duty, playing bass with them on the tour and whipping the road band into terrific shape.) America wanted to believe in the Beach Boys again, even kids who were too young ever to know that a Beach Boy was once in the full flush of his season. Traditionally, they had celebrated the wine of youth instead of the brittle roots of age. Now and forevermore, they would be the men who would be Beach Boys.

Brian's behavior worsened, and threatened to result in one dead Beach Boy. For ten long years the Beach Boys family had pretended that Brian was troubled but, well, "just Brian." After his breakdown in the mid-sixties was followed by two others, there is no report of psychiatric counseling, and one suspects that it simply didn't fit into the world view fostered by Hawthorne. Years later a friend persuaded Brian to visit a psychiatrist; when the family wouldn't hear of it, Brian went anyway, but the doctor was convinced his environment was the problem and refused to treat him as an outpatient. That was impossible: Brian would never leave home. Another friend shrugged with exasperation: "You've ultimately got to be an even greater genius than Brian at his best to really help the guy—and even then it could turn out to be a twenty-four-hour-a-day job."

"I'm not rehabilitating him," said Dr. Eugene E. Landy, a psychotherapist enlisted by Marilyn to help her husband, "I'm habilitating him. I'm re-parenting him, because the father he had beat the crap out of him." Landy was as much of a California creation as the Beach Boys—he dropped out of school when he was twelve, worked in the record business in his twenties, earned a psychology degree at thirty, and followed it with a Ph.D. Establishing a reputation working with dope-addled teenagers, he subsequently moved on to similarly troubled celebrities. His methods were unorthodox: twenty-four-hour-a-

---

In his personal liner notes on *All Summer Long,*
Dennis might as well have been saying goodbye:
"They say I live a fast life . . . It won't last forever,
either, but the memories will . . . I'll see you in your
town."

day therapy, wherein surrogates live with the patient and institute a program to reestablish a normal lifestyle. For Brian, Landy prescribed a diet and exercise program to get him back into shape, and a strict schedule of writing sessions. Like everybody from Murry to Jack Rieley, Landy aimed to integrate Brian back into the Beach Boys.

In 1976, with three years passed from their last original album, the Beach Boys needed a new product to celebrate their fifteenth anniversary and keep their revival alive. Brian would produce the LP, and to let him get his feet wet it would be composed of the kind of songs he and Mike used to sing along with on the radio. With Landy's encouragement—and his constant presence—Brian also spoke to the press, publicly lancing the boils he'd nurtured during his reclusive years. Between the recording and the public reckoning, the message was emphatic: Brian is back, and old fans rekindled hopes that had been long dormant. An NBC special was produced about the group that included a comedy bit wherein John Belushi and Dan Ackroyd, dressed as highway patrolmen, arrested Brian for failure to surf and forced him to wade into the choppy Pacific in search of the perfect wave. The oldies album *15 Big Ones* was released, and if it was produced with a lack of grace that matched its limited ambitions, old fans ignored the warning signs. Late in the year, Brian appeared on "Saturday Night Live" and sang a ragged solo version of "Good Vibrations" on a piano set in a—sandbox. Behind the camera, Landy, who had basked in the publicity surrounding the treatment of his star patient, directed Brian's performance. That night, old dreams died again.

Landy was subsequently dismissed—reportedly for reasons of expense and his intrusion into the group's affairs—but the product of his treatment was 1977's *Beach Boys Love You*. According to Carl, the LP was basically the rough demos of Brian's new songs that the two brothers produced at the group's Santa Monica recording studio. To unsympathetic ears the album sounds unduly

PRECEDING SPREAD:

**Shawn and Dennis with Gage at the World Music
Festival in Montego Bay, Jamaica, four months after
their July 1982 marriage.**

lightweight, and the lyrics simple-minded. The melodies, however, were a minor revelation, with tracks like "The Night Was So Young" offering proof that Brian's gift was intact, if shamelessly undisciplined. "Johnny Carson," debatably the kookiest song in the whole Beach Boys catalog, was so dry it was droll. Fans of Brian heard their old friend on *Beach Boys Love You,* and if he wasn't the aural sophisticate he once was, there was a chilling charm to these simple songs that suggested that he'd indeed reentered a childlike state during Dr. Landy's tenure.

"Live, from New York, it's Saturday Night!"
(November 27, 1976); Officer Brian confronts an
East Coast girl (Laraine Newman) before climbing
into the sandbox to ruin the "Good Vibrations."

FOLLOWING THEIR MID-SEVENTIES RENAISSANCE AND A LUCRA-tive recording deal that found the group moving from Warners to CBS, the Beach Boys' momentum splintered. Dennis completed a solo album that he'd been planning since *Sunflower,* Carl released the first of two solo records, Mike produced an album and toured with a mock-Beach Boys group called Celebration, and Brian sank back into his self-destructive habits. With the exception of Al, who played the happily married country gentleman along California's northern coast, personal lives were in tatters. The longtime marriages of Brian and Carl were both in their last stages. Dennis was into his second marriage (making a total of four) to Karen Lamm, and like the first, it was falling victim to a predilection for booze and cocaine. One day Dennis drove Karen's Ferrari down to Venice Beach, doused its interior with lighter fluid, and torched it. As it burned, he walked to a nearby house and played the piano. The group was not one big happy family, and for a time in 1977 the Beach Boys appeared to have broken up. On one side there were Mike and Al, who had become a full corporate member of the group in the mid-seventies; Carl and Dennis held down the Wilson end of the Beach Boys, with Brian's pivotal vote often an abstention. At one point, however, Brian inexplicably tendered his support to Mike, who promptly fired all nonmeditating members of the band and threatened to replace Carl and Dennis. (Dennis, deeper still into drugs and drink, had become a problematic participant in concert tours, and was periodically barred from Beach Boys shows.) Passions cooled, as they customarily have when the bottom line was involved, but the group remained a shaky and simmering alliance. Bruce Johnston, who had left the band during the Rieley period and gone on to write (we always knew he had it in him) Barry Manilow's "I Write the Songs," was brought back to lend stability. No matter: when Dennis began a late-seventies affair with Shawn Love, Mike's sixteen-year-old illegitimate daughter, the bad blood spilled into an open feud. On tour, bodyguards kept Dennis away from the bottle before the show, and Mike and Dennis apart after the show—and a court order was eventually needed to keep the men apart. Regardless, the past has a habit of repeating itself; Shawn gave birth, and Dennis's illegitimate son became Mike's illegitimate grandson. Then, the brother married the cousin's daughter.

America can't let go of the Beach Boys and the youthful notions that they held in their harmonies. Brian's songs sing to a particularly American innocence that may never be quite grasped, but is never impossibly far from reach. That's why, deep into the eighties, they remain summer annuals in broadcast advertising: the Beach Boys chronicled a consumer society with music of spiritual depth. Theirs is a land of milk and wild honey. Good, good, good, good vibrations. Brian's songs didn't attain this emotional effervescence by a blind compulsion to look on the bright side; it just never occurred to him to create anything less than the beautiful. Some perceive the Beach Boys' lack of a dark side as an artistic flaw, which may say more about the times than the songs. Yet it's significant that their insistently sunny vibe is what's prevented decades of dirty laundry from soiling the integrity of Brian's noble body of work. Like the Beach Boys, we need those songs. James Watt knew none of this in 1983 when, in his position as Secretary of the Interior, he denied permission for the Beach Boys to perform a Fourth of July concert on the Mall of the nation's capital, and claimed that they would attract an undesirable element. The incident was headline news not just because of the chronically lose lips that eventually drove Watt from his job, but because a sizable number of citizens could instantly see that he knew nothing about the America in which they lived. By contrast, President Reagan is a scholar of American image, and had a visceral

OVERLEAF:

Brian listens for the music in his head, but some who love him wonder if his mind has been dulled to the sound. Dr. Landy looks over the shoulder of his star patient.

understanding of the Beach Boys. Though musical visionaries, they have consistently complemented the middle-class culture. In nine years they had gone from playing May Day to a benefit for George Bush. The Beach Boys are Reagan's kind of rock band. They symbolize a be-true-to-your-school kind of America where fun is guaranteed to the privileged, and the lonely losers better watch their ass.

Brian Wilson sits in his room, one of Landy's lackeys for company. He was given an ultimatum by the group in 1982: return to Landy's care, or be fired from the group. Brian was broke, and had no choice; he pays Landy a reported fifty thousand dollars a month. Brian whispers the lyric that he says is closest to his heart. "When I find myself in times of trouble, Mother Mary comforts me." It's the Beatles, not the Beach Boys; Paul, not Brian. What's more, it's a song produced by Phil Spector. "Speaking words of wisdom, let it be." In the fall of 1983, brother Dennis is on a high dive. He has no money, and won't be permitted to tour with the group until he's cleaned himself up. He checks in and out of de-tox centers. Dennis has no home—he's divorced Shawn, who's moved with their son into a single room—and crashes with friends. On December 28, in Marina del Rey, Dennis, the only real Beach Boy, is hanging out on a friend's boat drinking vodka and diving off an adjoining pier. The water is 58 degrees—wet-suit weather, but the Beach Boy is swimming in cutoffs. He drowns in twelve feet of murky water. The Reagans arrange for Dennis to be buried at sea.

July 4, 1984, Washington, D.C. The Beach Boys are back in Washington, redeemed, reinstated—they are America's band. The business wheels have been working overtime; their return to the Mall is the most attention they have gotten since that dreadful drowning. A few nights earlier they appeared on

When Brian lost Marilyn and his daughters to divorce, he was left with the family he would never leave—the Beach Boys.

OVERLEAF:

Carl enjoying a domestic respite between concert stops on the endless summer.

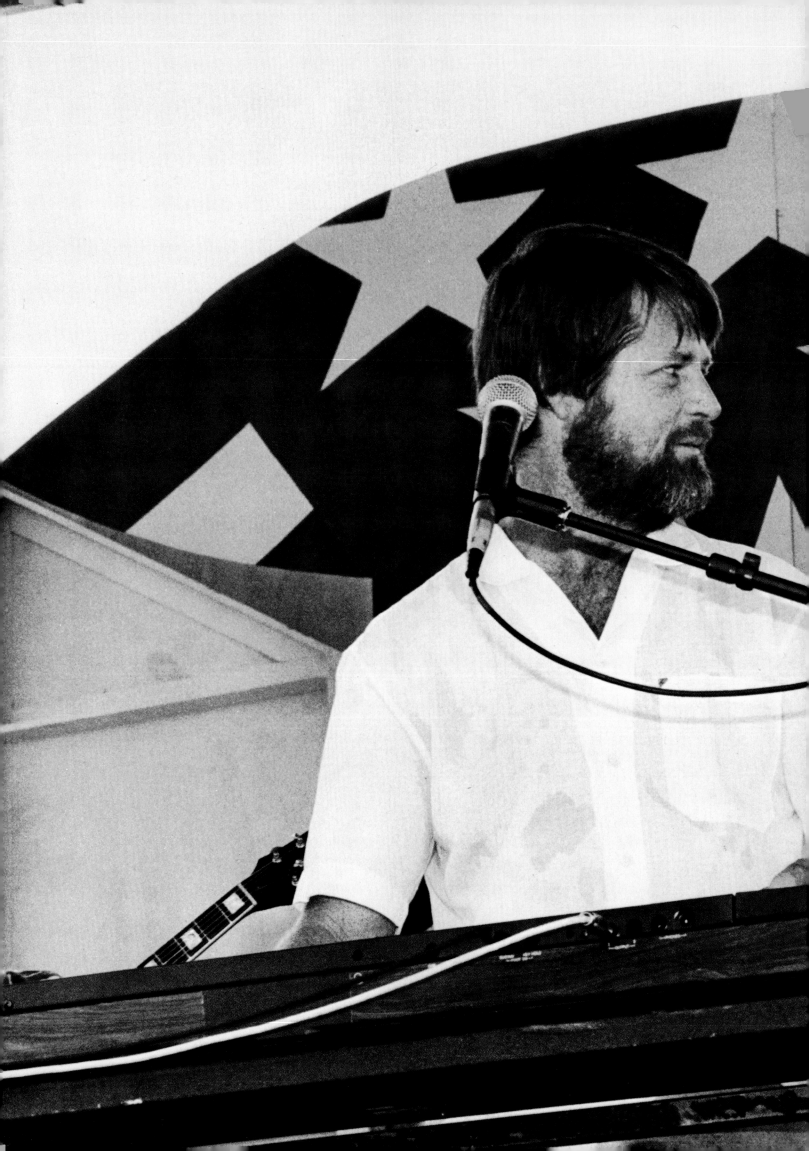

"The Tonight Show" and Joan Rivers asked Brian how he'd lost so much weight. Brian credited his "therapist, manager, and songwriter," Eugene Landy. Landy will reportedly write new material with Brian, entitling him to royalties, though whether his participation will be to simply make Brian sit down at the piano or actually collaborate on the songs is unclear. But for now Landy's center stage, with an orange T-shirt that says "The Perfect Nut!" and a financial stake in the Beach Boys. Brian and Landy run from trailer to trailer, getting earplugs here and commemorative T-shirts there, and dodging the video cameras that are putting a wrap on a full-length video on the history of the group. As always, it's the Beach Boys' past that's being sold: Brian in his firemen's hat, creating bad vibrations; Brian in his sandbox, singing "Good Vibrations"; Brian and the Beach Boys, creating an enduring vibration. Steve Levine, a hot young British record producer, is backstage taking in the colonial atmosphere before heading into the studio to try to give the group some contemporary life. Julio Iglesias, who's just used the Beach Boys on his recording of "The Air That I Breathe," pinches Brian's cheek and calls him a genius.

It's Independence Day, and Brian Wilson is onstage before a crowd of people that stretches as far as the eye can see. From his seat at an electric piano, turned way down in case he starts playing a different song, he can look out at the Washington Monument standing tall and proud. It's some incredible sight from that piano. All those people. Americans of all shapes and sizes, moving to those songs that he wrote so long ago. Those songs too stand tall—a man could build something with them, one on top of another: "I Get Around" and "Fun, Fun, Fun," "The Warmth of the Sun" and "Surf's Up," *Pet Sounds* and *Sunflower*. Enduring, spiritual music, fashioned with love and secured with the mortar of brotherly harmony. It will be a lovely monument, built right here on the Mall, with "Surfin' U.S.A." and "California Girls," "Good Vibrations" and "Don't

Carl makes a funny face at his older brother. People
have talked about Brian's condition for so long that
they often slip into the past tense.

Worry Baby," and "God Only Knows" what else. We'll plant palm trees in front, and invite this whole world to come to the dedication and celebrate the news: a great American artist lives in our hearts. Murry will be there, and he'll bust his buttons with pride, and throw his arms around his son and tell him that he loves him. Then it'll be time to cut the ribbon, and the TV news will jockey for good camera angles. Brian will revel in the moment, but he'll melt when he sees her blond hair in the crowd, and damn near cry when she walks up to him like some angel of mercy. Then, with all the world watching, Wendy will stretch upward and kiss him on the lips, and for now and evermore, Brian will wear a smile.

OVERLEAF:

Then (1975, with Jim Guercio on bass), now, and
forevermore, the Beach Boys are an American band.

Secretary of the Interior James Watt claimed that the
Beach Boys would attract an "undesirable element"
to the Fourth of July festivities on the Washington,
D.C., Mall, so he went to Las Vegas for Wayne
Newton. The next year, Watt was out, the Beach
Boys were back, and Dennis was dead. Later that
summer, after the Beach Boys entertained a kick-off
party at the 1984 Republican Convention in Dallas,
Brian was arrested for being in the convention hall
without proper accreditation, and quickly released.
In the sunshine of his youth, Brian wrote rock and
roll for an America that President Reagan would
recognize as his own.

233

The Beach Boys depend on their past and the kindness of strangers. In Washington they are joined by Ringo Starr, the drummer from that other "Bea" group, for a version of the Beatles' tribute to the Beach Boys, "Back in the U.S.S.R."; international singing star Julio Iglesias used the opportunity to make a video of "The Air That I Breathe"; and Mike Love hugs First Fan Nancy Reagan. The crowd had the warmth of the sun, and as sad as their story might be, the Beach Boys have brought the same to you and me.

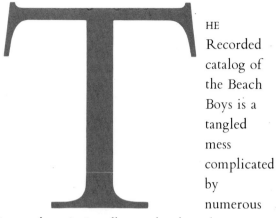

HE Recorded catalog of the Beach Boys is a tangled mess complicated by numerous reissues, late sixties albums that have been distributed by two major labels, and LPs from the seventies that are already long out of print. Litigation between the group and Capitol gave both parties control over the five albums between **PET SOUNDS** and **20/20**; consequently, they have been marketed by both Capitol (in original release and subsequent budget lines) and Warner Brothers (in bargain twofers). That still doesn't explain the unbelievable fate of **PET SOUNDS**. Sixteen years after its release Capitol called Warners to see if they could pool their cumulative sales figures and squeak out a gold album. No go! When the Beach Boys carried their catalog with them to CBS in the late seventies, their Warners material fell out of circulation. **SUNFLOWER** (my copy crackles and pops from fifteen years of play) and **SURF'S UP** are both out of print; most of what was worthy was included on a 1981 CBS compilation, **TEN YEARS OF HARMONY**, also unavailable.

From the Beatles on down, **GREATEST HITS** collections have been regarded as aesthetically tacky ways in which to enjoy and understand a band's true breadth and importance. The Beach Boys, of course, preceded both the Beatles and the time when the album became the state of the art. The name of their game was hot hits and harmonies, and their success was built on singles, not albums. There's no way around it; the first two of three two-record compilations Capitol released to multi-platinum euphoria in the mid-seventies constitute the basic Beach Boys:

☆ **ENDLESS SUMMER**—These two records contain virtually all (from "Surfin' Safari" to "California Girls") of Brian Wilson's major summertime hits. Released in 1974, it allowed a still-strong live band to clean up financially, and further ensured that these men would spend their lives playing boys. Their past, and ours as well, remains a great pleasure—add a bit of sunshine, or at least an open window, and these songs are a cheap and easy day at the beach.

☆ **SPIRIT OF AMERICA**—The pickings got slimmer for Capitol's 1975 double set, which draws largely from the excellent **TODAY** and includes such essentials as "Please Let Me Wonder" and "When I Grow Up (To Be A Man)." Other highlights are unavailable elsewhere, including the super-cool flop-single follow-up to "California Girls," "The Little Girl I Once Knew," and the schmaltzy summer-of-'69 tune Brian wrote with Murry, "Break Away."

Purists might argue that these albums take songs out of their proper context; realists will admit that their context doesn't exist anymore anyway. Still, Capitol's budget-line reissues of early Beach Boys albums do the group a not-so-subtle injustice—there's just too little poetry in renaming **SUMMER DAYS (AND SUMMER NIGHTS)** after "California Girls." Similarly, deletions deny the albums their historic purity; in the case of **TODAY** (retitled **DANCE, DANCE, DANCE**), a juggling of songs destroys that album's special yin-yang character. Still, these two and **ALL SUMMER LONG** capture the heyday of upper-case Fun, and include personal notes from all the

guys (and Dick Clark too).

☆ **PET SOUNDS**—It's a cultural crime that this album never went gold. Invited to dinner? Take **PET SOUNDS** in lieu of a bottle of wine. Send it to your first love, or your last. Maybe if we think and wish and hope and pray, this classic will finally sell its worth, and Brian will let loose with that long-overdue follow-up. Sure, just like Banana and Louie are going to stop chasing that train. Thunk—a true desert island album—thunk.

Beach Boys albums of the late sixties all have their moments; their common disappointment remains that none of them was **SMILE**. The one solution, beautiful even in its obscurity, is to do what Brian never did: make a tape of **SMILE** using the pieces the Beach Boys scattered from 1967's **SMILEY SMILE** to 1972's **SURF'S UP**. Bootleg albums and tapes give the **SMILE** chronicler a distinct advantage, but an extraordinary LP's worth of music is commercially available. In deference to Brian, I believe that everybody's **SMILE** tape should be different, but can't resist recommending the basic drift of mine, beginning with "Heroes and Villains" and winding up in the spiritual ozone of "Cabinessence," "Our Prayer," and "Surf's Up." (A 1983 Capitol release, **RARITIES**, allows you to spice up your tape with an alternate take of "Good Vibrations" and "You're Welcome," a piece of rhythmic chanting available only as the B-side of "Heroes and Villains." Another highlight is a version of a song from, of all things, **SGT. PEPPER**—"With a Little Help From My Friends.")

SUNSHINE BELIEVER, the third of Capitol's double sets, collects from **PET SOUNDS** through **20/20**, and the mix is necessarily strained. A cost-efficient way to cover a lot of bases, it nonetheless ignores the fact that during the late sixties each new Beach Boys album boasted a whole new feel. Consequently a song like "Darlin'" will always sound best in the context of **WILD HONEY**, whereas an earlier piece like "Fun, Fun, Fun" lost nothing by standing alone. The gangly "Beach Boys Medley" is the compilation's own bad review. Warners released twin packs pairing **SMILEY SMILE/FRIENDS** and **WILD HONEY/20-20**, which are excellent buys in a used or out-of-print record bin. Otherwise they are budget-lined by Capitol with the original covers and no songs deleted. All are individually worthwhile, essential for constructing a relatively complete **SMILE** tape, and ranked in descending order by my own taste:

☆ **WILD HONEY** (1967)—The Beach Boys cut a roughhouse band album over at Brian's home studio, with a slate of songs by Brian and Mike that explored the r&b roots that had always been fairly well hidden. "Wild Honey" and "Darlin'" steal the show, with "Country Air" offering bucolic competition and "I Was Made to Love Her" as the only serious misfire. One distressing note: this is the LP on which Carl began to sing the leads formerly handled by his older brother.

☆ **FRIENDS** (1968)—This is the Beach Boys' folkie album—more accurately, their Transcendental Meditation LP—and it boasts a warmth that is quietly compelling. The title tune, "Wake The World," and "Anna Lee, The Healer" evoke a mood that is equal parts campfire and hymnal. Brian's "Busy Doin' Nothin'" captures the sleepy state of his spirit.

☆ **20/20** (1969)—The group's last album for Capitol, there is no reason that its grab-bag of odds and ends should hang together, but it does. Besides including two **SMILE** essentials

("Cabinessence" and "Our Prayer"), the LP also features "Do It Again" (and again), a wonderful Spector cover sung by Carl, "I Can Hear Music," and an oddly psychedelic "Bluebirds Over The Mountain."

☆ SMILEY SMILE (1967)—More than any late sixties Beach Boys album, this one suffers from not being SMILE. Where the original album was to have featured dense and sophisticated tracks topped by harmonic meringue, the LP that belatedly emerged took some of the same material to minimalist extremes. The best tunes are essential in any form obtainable— "Wonderful," "Wind Chimes," "Heroes and Villains," "Vege-Tables," "Good Vibrations"— but the knowledge of what's missing irrevocably tinges what's there.

For a record buyer in the eighties, the Beach Boys of the seventies hardly exist. Not only is their Warners product out of print, but sales were so meager for their new CBS material that it too disappeared from record stores. For diehards who contend that the Beach Boys have never lost their contemporary (as opposed to timeless) appeal, this shocking hole in their catalog shuts down all arguments. The Beach Boys have always existed to make popular music; the fact that a twenty-five-year-old album remains in print while one a half-dozen years old is unavailable speaks for itself. With a little luck, however, the diligent shopper might be rewarded with finding copies of these notable releases:

☆ SUNFLOWER (1970)—The Beach Boys go Hollywood with an album sweet enough to serve for dessert. Brian's voice is hardly to be heard, but his influence is felt throughout, in both the vocal arrangements and the rich mix of instruments. With Dennis contributing four songs, SUNFLOWER is also the home of his best work.

☆ SURF'S UP (1971)—Lacking the sophisticated follow-through of SUNFLOWER, the LP nonetheless succeeded on the strength of two of Brian's finest songs ("Surf's Up" and "Until I Die"), and Carl's greatest hits ("Feel Flows" and "The Trader"). Also included is either Brian's all-time worst song or best practical joke, "A Day in the Life of a Tree," which leaves one longing for an ax.

☆ BEACH BOYS LOVE YOU (1977)—Brian's post-therapy LP in which the listener is invited into the sandbox. A fascinating record which proved that Brian had never lost his facility with melodies, only the will to translate them into completed productions. Though Brian sings in a voice more sour than sweet, songs like "The Night Was So Young" and "Solar System" leave us nonetheless mourning for more. Brian's comic classic, "Johnny Carson," finds him thunderstruck at how Johnny keeps it up night after night. Like Brian, we laugh to keep from crying.

The CBS compilation TEN YEARS OF HARMONY includes the best tracks from SUNFLOWER, SURF'S UP, and the highlights from such mediocre efforts as HOLLAND, M.I.U., and L.A. (LIGHT ALBUM). As the Beach Boys retain the rights to all of this work, there's always the possibility for future rereleases and, yes, new albums as well. But as any true Beach Boys fan has learned, one risks disappointment by expecting too much. It's okay to wish for something as lovely as "God Only Knows," or as flat-out fun as "I Get Around," but if it never comes, it's nice to know what can never go away.

My primary source material for this aesthetic biography was the music of the Beach Boys. To fill out the story of their music, I was faced with a choice: either interview the Beach Boys (who refused my request) and all of their associates for the past twenty-five years or absorb the existing Beach Boys reportage into my critical analysis. As my aim was music criticism and not muckraking, I chose the latter; moreover, I felt that the classically dramatic arc of their tragic story said as much as the dirty specifics. (Ultimately I spent an hour with Carl, to whom I owe thanks, along with his personal manager Jerry Schilling. As follow-ups would have been needed for true depth, I regarded our conversation as deep background.) While I read other articles and reviews during the course of my research, those cited in the following narrative bibliography are those that have influenced my text. To these authors and to all the others who've chronicled the life and times of this American band, I owe a debt of thanks.

The literature of the Beach Boys parallels the growth of rock writing itself. When they began, there was no such thing as a rock critic; if the music was covered at all, it was with the purple prose of a teenage fan magazine. If any establishment publication deigned to cover a concert, it was a dog duty given to a general-assignment reporter who treated it as some kind of alien teenage rite. As late as the arrival of the Beatles, the established media were trying to explain away the phenomenon and to deny what teenage America already knew—rock and roll, Pops, was here to stay.

Paul Williams is widely regarded as one of the very first rock writers. He began by publishing a mimeographed sheet about rock and roll inspired by the folk publication SING OUT, which grew into the first serious rock magazine, CRAWDADDY. Williams was quick to look beyond the striped shirts and understand the significance of PET SOUNDS, both in terms of the Beach Boys and the growing sophistication of pop music. His lengthy interview with David Anderle, reprinted in his book OUTLAW BLUES, offers a view into the SMILE period from the perspective of a former insider still smarting from the experience. (The amusing flip-flop both men take on WILD HONEY could be the first documented example of rock-crit revisionism.)

Almost everything written about the SMILE era goes ga-ga over the fact that Jules Siegel wrenched an assignment out of his editors at THE SATURDAY EVENING POST to write about the Beach Boys. The article—"Goodbye Surfing, Hello God!"—was eventually rejected by the POST but surfaced in another early rock magazine, CHEETAH, and is the single best picture of Brian at the crossroads of his life. (The piece can be found in a collection of Siegel's work, RECORD, published by Straight Arrow Press.) In the context of Hollywood coming to Hawthorne (or, in this case, Manhattan coming to Manhattan Beach), the piece is an erudite case in point. Siegel understood and appreciated Brian's artistry and had come to pay him tribute, which is probably why the POST passed on the story. But by the time Siegel had examined his subject,

he was left with the sad spectacle of an artist lost in his own aspirations and a brother who was deeply dependent on the family from whom he was increasingly alienated. Brian's life simply couldn't withstand the attention that he craved; ultimately, the piece was the journalistic equivalent of Paul McCartney saying "God Only Knows" was the best pop song ever written. Brian was having a hard enough time saying goodbye to surfing, let alone saying hello to God.

During the hippie heyday of the late sixties, the Beach Boys were all but ignored by the burgeoning rock press. ROLLING STONE, publishing out of San Francisco, profiled their Bay Area brethren and pooh-poohed the band that meant California to the rest of the world. (For information concerning Charles Manson, Ed Sanders' THE FAMILY and Vincent Bugliosi and Curt Gentry's HELTER SKELTER were helpful.) In 1971, responding to the group's critical revival after the release of SUNFLOWER, the magazine published "The Beach Boys: A California Saga," a two-part story by Tom Nolan (with additional material by David Felton) that for the first time threw daylight on the whole ugly can of worms. Everything written about the group after 1971 drew on Nolan's exemplary work, and while the piece was notable for its primary sources (including Murry and Nick Venet), its true power came from the understated sympathy that informed Nolan's prose.

In the years that followed, little was seen in print on the Beach Boys, a reflection of their low commercial esteem and, perhaps, their reticence after the ROLLING STONE pieces. As a group based on the concept of family, the Beach Boys have always kept outsiders at a distance; similarly, as men who like their money, they've accepted public scrutiny when the price was

right. Following their in-concert revival on the nostalgic strength of ENDLESS SUMMER and SPIRIT OF AMERICA, the group knew it needed to reestablish their contemporary credibility and turned to the guy who had always made them tick. A campaign was organized and the message was this: "Brian is back!" To promote his "comeback" album, 1976's desultory 15 BIG ONES, Brian met the press, who wolfed down his tragic story with gusto. A new character had been added to the script, Brian's twenty-four-hour-a-day therapist Eugene Landy, who considered Brian's public exorcism a significant part of his treatment.

David Felton stitched a series of interviews into ROLLING STONE's "The Healing of Brother Bri," a piece whose knowing portrait of Brian denied its title. Tim White wrote a two-part piece for CRAWDADDY that caught the spirit of the group's heyday, dug up instances of the emasculation of Brian during the dark days, and finally, like the naïve lover to which all true Beach Boys fans bear a resemblance, agreed that Brian was indeed back. Writing in NEW WEST, Steven Gaines concentrated on Brian's therapy with Landy. Across the Big Pond, the British music papers did multipart pieces on the group, with Nick Kent writing a particularly well-informed three-parter in NEW MUSIC EXPRESS and Richard Cromelin contributing a two-parter to SOUNDS.

Building on these sources and on his own extensive reporting, David Leaf wrote the first authoritative biography of the group, THE BEACH BOYS AND THE CALIFORNIA MYTH (Grosset & Dunlap). Culling information from a wide network of principals and associates, Leaf paints a sympathetic appreciation of their work and painful downfall. Leaf makes no bones about his

belief that Brian Wilson is the raison d'être of the Beach Boys and, much in the manner of the Nolan pieces that he cites as an inspiration, we can practically hear Leaf's heart break under the weight of his accumulated documentation. For his thorough integration of Beach Boys literature, as well as his own reporting, I am particularly indebted to Leaf's book which, unlike **SUNFLOWER,** has been reissued (retitled **SPIRIT OF AMERICA**) after falling out of print.

THE BEACH BOYS, by Byron Preiss (St. Martin's Press) was an authorized biography of the band that was presumably intended to be a counterstrike against the more truthful account offered in Leaf's book. Drawing again on the accumulated Beach Boys literature, Preiss also based his work on additional interviews with the band. The presentation is less than artful, with blocks of boldface quotes and lyrics dropped into Preiss's prose; more damaging are the dramatic blind spots that are predictable given the book's "authorized" status. Interestingly, Preiss goes into **SMILE** at some length, indicating that the band doesn't mind milking their fans' interest in their legendary cop-out. The book, which was revised in 1983 and reissued with much less artwork, also includes an extensive discography.

As the seventies waned, so did press coverage of the Beach Boys, who slipped back into the netherworld of nostalgia. In 1978 John Swenson wrote in **ROLLING STONE** about the group's on-again, off-again breakup and the newspapers made much of the James Watt flap in 1983. The death of Dennis Wilson prompted a sordid story by Michael Goldberg in **ROLLING STONE,** and **PEOPLE** did a characteristically thorough postmortem. The reunion of Dr. Landy and his star patient prompted Jerry Lazar to write a piece for **CALIFORNIA** magazine. Of the

numerous critics who've written about the music of the Beach Boys, I found reviews written by Jim Miller and Ken Barnes to be the most insightful.

On the personal front, I'm ever grateful to my California host, Chuck Stepner, who never seems to mind, no matter how long I stay. Dinner with the Golden State's own Bobbi Cowan helped me get a fix on growing up in L.A. in the fifties. Breakfast with Gene Sculatti, Beach Boys aficionado and longtime chronicler of California music, was similarly helpful, as was lunch and a long walk through Santa Monica with David Leaf. Tom Vickers kept my head clear by running me around the tennis court and also shared his collection of Four Freshmen records and videotapes of Brian and the boys rocking out on mid-sixties TV. Bob Merlis of Warner Bros. saved me hours of library research by letting me peruse his publicity files; Glen Brunman of CBS facilitated my meeting with Carl; Maureen O'Connor of Capitol freshened up my collection of classic Beach Boys albums. Thanks as well to Andy Frances, who copped me a **SMILE** bootleg; Danny Hutton, who sent me a snatch of same that sounded "just like jewelry"; and Jack Schechtman, who helped me listen to the Beach Boys through the ears of a musician.

Two conversations were particularly helpful for my own morale and confidence. I met Van Dyke Parks in New York while he was promoting his excellent **JUMP** LP and followed up over a late afternoon bottle of California wine. "To look at an elephant," he counseled, "it's often best to step back." Then he added, "But how will you leave them laughing?" Upon completing the manuscript, I profiled Lindsey Buckingham of Fleetwood Mac, a well-known fan of Brian Wilson who enjoyed "a window"

into the workings of the band while fellow-Mac Christine McVie was going out with Dennis. Predictably, we spent most of our time talking about the Beach Boys (Buckingham had just released a tribute to Dennis and the group, "D. W. Suite") and our impressions were in perfect harmony.

Thanks to Billy Altman, Dave Marsh, and Paul Jellinek, who each gave the manuscript a careful reading and offered valuable advice. I'm ever grateful to my agent Carol Mann, whose mind is as sharp as her backhand, for introducing me to my editor at Dolphin/ Doubleday, Jim Fitzgerald, who knows how to put rock and roll between the covers of a book. Thanks too to J. C. Suarés, for the spiffy design, Casey Fuetsch for keeping the ball rolling, and Chaucy Bennetts and Mark Hurst for conscientious copy editing. And finally, thanks to my sister Connie, for love and support beyond the call of family, and Ilene Cherna, who, besides pulling together the book's photos, made the whole project feel like fun.

Photo Credits

Page 1 The Peter Reum Collection; **2–3** Collage by Jim Fitzgerald, Photos by Jasper Dailey from The Peter Reum Collection; **4** Max Aguilera-Hellweg; **6** Warner Brothers; **7** The Peter Reum Collection; **9, 11, 13, 15, 17** Alan Bergman; **18** The Peter Reum Collection; **21, 22–23, 24, 25** Rich Sloan/The Peter Reum Collection; **29** Pictorial Press Ltd.; **30, 32** The Peter Reum Collection; **34** Edward Vandegrift; **35** The Peter Reum Collection; **36, 37** Michael Ochs Archives; **38–39, 42, 43, 45** The Peter Reum Collection; **46** Michael Ochs Archives; **47** The Peter Reum Archives; **62** Pictorial Press Ltd.; **64–65** The Peter Reum Collection; **67** Julian Wasser; **69, 70–71** Michael Ochs Archives; **72–73** Julian Wasser; **75** Dezo Hoffmann/RDR Productions; **78, 79** Julian Wasser; **80** Bill Ray, LIFE magazine, ©1965 Time Inc.; **82–83** UPI/ Bettmann Archive; **86–87** Pictorial Press Ltd.; **88** Guy Webster; **90–91** Globe Photos; **94–95** Pictorial Press Ltd.; **98–99** Dezo Hoffmann/ RDR Productions; **102–103** Julian Wasser; **105, 106–107** Dezo Hoffman/RDR Productions; **110, 111** The Peter Reum Collection; **115** Pictorial Press Ltd; **117** Guy Webster; **118–19** Garry Sato; **121** Bob Jenkins; **124** David Hiller; **125** David Hiller/The Peter Reum Collection; **127** Guy Webster; **130** Les Chan; **131** Guy Webster/The Peter Reum Collection; **132** Bob Jenkins; **134–35** Lois Greenfield; **139** Bob Jenkins; **140, 141** Lois Greenfield; **143** Bob Jenkins; **144–45** Jim Marshall; **148–49** John R. Hamilton/Globe Photos; **152–53** Bob Jenkins; **156–57, 158–59, 160–61, 162–63, 164–65** Julian Wasser; **166** Chris Walter/Retna Ltd.; **169** Michael Zagaris; **170–71** Julian Wasser; **173** Dean O. Torrence; **174, 175, 176–77** Julian Wasser; **179** Gary Nichoman; **180** Ebet Roberts; **181** John Bellissimo/Retna Ltd.; **182–83** Mark Sennet/Gamma-Liaison; **185** Julian Wasser; **186–87** Michael Zagaris; **191** Alan Bergman; **194–95** Guy Webster; **196–97** Annie Leibovitz/Contact; **199, 200–1** Neal Preston/ Camera 5; **203** Alan Bergman; **206, 207** Neal Preston/Camera 5; **209** Julian Wasser; **210–11** John Bellissimo/Retna Ltd.; **216–17** Neal Preston/Camera 5; **219** Ray Amati; **220–21** Julian Wasser; **222–23** Ebet Roberts; **226–27** Barry Bregman/Gamma-Liaison; **228–29** AP/ Wide World Photos; **230 top** Ebet Roberts; **230 bottom** AP/Wide World Photos; **231** UPI/ Bettmann Archive; **232** Julian Wasser.